C000042366

Democracy and the Fall
of the West

Craig Smith and Tom Miers

SOCIETAS
essays in political
& cultural criticism

imprint-academic.com

Copyright © Craig Smith and Tom Miers, 2011

The moral rights of the author have been asserted.
No part of this publication may be reproduced in any form
without permission, except for the quotation of brief passages
in criticism and discussion.

Published in the UK by Societas
Imprint Academic, PO Box 200, Exeter EX5 5YX, UK

Published in the USA by Societas
Imprint Academic, Philosophy Documentation Center
PO Box 7147, Charlottesville, VA 22906-7147, USA

ISBN 9781845402150

A CIP catalogue record for this book is available from the
British Library and US Library of Congress

Contents

Introduction — Illiberal Democracy   1

1   The Struggle for Liberty   3

2   Warnings from the Past   17

3   Democracy and the Abuse of Law   33

4   Democracy and the Big State   49

5   The Return of Market Liberalism   67

6   The Fall of the West   79

Epilogue — An Idea for the Future   97

Bibliography   100

Introduction

Illiberal Democracy

This book sets out a hypothesis: that modern democracy is leading to a new tyranny, undermining the foundations of the West's success in a way that will inevitably cause its decline and fall.

Democracy is commonly thought of as one of the linchpins of the West—a key component that guarantees the freedoms, identity and dynamism of Western society. We contend the opposite: that the concept of a 'liberal democracy' is a contradiction in terms. The democratic process unleashes political forces that increase the power of the state at the expense of liberty to the point where democratic government is little different in outcome to the other forms of tyranny that exist and have existed around the world.

The idea of democracy being inimical to liberty is not new. In fact the potential problems inherent in democratic government have been discussed by some of the greatest Western philosophers from classical times onwards. The first chapter of this book sets out the central features of liberalism[1] that are the foundations of Western success. In Chapter Two we'll look at the place of democracy in the development of Western political thought and show the ambivalence, and at times downright hostility of some of the greatest of Western political thinkers to the idea of

[1]   In this book the word 'liberal' holds its original meaning pertaining to individual liberty, rather than its occasional modern political usage (especially in the United States) meaning 'left wing'.

democracy. In Chapter Three we will trace the tension between the idea of law and the demands of democracy, showing how the growth of democratic government has subtly undermined the notion of the rule of law.

Modern political classes are not entirely blind to the problems thrown up by democratic government. Chapter Four describes the material consequences of democratic socialism while Chapter Five tells the story of the liberal reaction against this. But while democratic politicians may identify the flaws in socialism and act to remedy them, their efforts are doomed by the political system in which they operate. Chapter Six shows how the West is now losing its special edge and returning to the normal condition of history — a state where powerful governments compete to achieve political goals at the expense of both the individual and civil society.

We end on a note of hope, however, imagining in the epilogue how we could finally construct a new form of governance that entrenches liberalism and constrains the power of government forever.

Political economy is never an exact science. This book does not attempt to justify in great detail the many historical, political and philosophical conclusions we draw. To do so would lengthen it beyond easy readability without proving our point. Even the concept of 'the West' is hard to define exactly. Many of our examples and references come from Britain. But the same trends are apparent in other countries with a strong tradition of both liberty and democracy.

So this book is not meant to be definitive. Instead we hope it outlines an unconventional idea in fairly short form with the aim of inviting readers to look at modern Western society more critically.

Chapter One

The Struggle
for Liberty

In May 2010 the United Kingdom held one of the periodic
rituals of its status as a democracy — a General Election. The
election was eagerly anticipated, partly as a result of the
longevity of the sitting government, partly because of the
corruption of the departing Parliament and partly because
of the economic problems facing the nation. The introduction of television debates between the party leaders repre-
sented the only real innovation in the campaign process.
The mechanics of an election are now familiar across the
globe and they were engaged in Britain with only some
minor misfires concerning postal voting and queues at clos-
ing polling stations.

The result of the election was a hung parliament and a
week of frantic negotiations to form a coalition that would
provide a stable government for the country. One result of
this chain of events, enhanced by the presence of the Liberal
Democrats in the resulting coalition, was an increased discussion of electoral reform and the extent to which Britain's
government was genuinely democratic. Widespread dissatisfaction with the policies of a particular government is
commonplace, but the events of the preceding few years
had led many in Britain to ask deeper questions about the
nature of their political constitution. Much of this discussion concerned itself with the possible permutations of
changing the electoral system or reforming the House of

Lords, but little of it addressed the deeper nature of the political system.

In this book we hope to confront precisely this issue — to ask the very difficult question of whether our deep commitment to the ideal of democratic politics has the potential to undermine the success of our way of life. This is not a problem limited to the United Kingdom. To the extent that what is known as the West is united by a shared commitment to democracy, so it too faces the deeper problems that we seek to address.

Democracy is often regarded as a universal value: the culmination of a set of historical developments in a collection of political societies that has come to be known as the West. The West has enjoyed unprecedented levels of economic growth and political power over the last 300 years. And it is over this same period that the countries of the West have developed their democratic polities. In the view of many this is no coincidence. Democracy and economic growth, coupled with political stability and a flourishing society, come together as a package arrived at by the West. The economic and social progress associated with the West has become a vindication of democracy — an argument that has allied itself to the moral argument for democracy as the only legitimate way of organising the political life of a nation.

That democracy is a good thing is now a near universally accepted tenet of political thinking in the West, and now beyond. Some two thirds of the world's states are now democratic. As democracy has spread around the world increasing numbers of people have been convinced that it is the key to a successful and flourishing society. So prevalent is this view that some have even come to consider it their moral duty to spread democracy around the world, to encourage or even enforce it where it has yet to take hold. In the face of this near universal admiration for democracy it runs the risk of becoming an unquestioned orthodoxy.

In this volume we want to pause and take a cool look at the notion of democracy. While we are not against elected governments *per se*, we feel that many of the benefits that have traditionally been associated with democracy are not the result of that political system. Instead they are the result of another dimension of the West's development. The simplest way to understand the point that we want to make is to realise that what is often referred to in casual conversation as a 'democracy' is actually more accurately described as 'liberal democracy'. The point of stressing this is that most of what is valuable in the political order achieved by the West is actually a result of its liberalism rather than its democracy.

Liberalism and democracy are intertwined in the political systems of the West and it is our contention that they are in serious tension, and that this tension has the potential to destabilise the Western nations and destroy the sources of their success.

*   *   *

Let's be clear from the start about what we mean by dividing the term 'liberal democracy' into two constituent concepts. There is a clear distinction between the two sets of political ideals and institutions — those of liberalism and those of democracy. Our contention is simple — that the tremendous success of the West over the last three hundred years has been a product of the liberalism of Western nations rather than of their commitment to democracy. We are not blind to the fact that democracy is a valuable part of the political structure developed in the West over this period, but we want to be clear about the source of the West's progress.

By liberalism we mean a set of ideals and institutions developed in the West over a long historical period. The chief institutional characteristics of liberalism include legal protection of individual rights and a sphere of private life, religious toleration, the limitation of political power by law and constitutions, the defence of property rights and the institutions of a market economy. These institutions are backed by commitment to human freedom as a moral and political value. By democracy we understand a form of political organisation characterised as rule by the people, in modern political systems via elected representatives. The institutions of democracy are accompanied by a wider set of beliefs about the value of egalitarian political order and the desirability of extending democracy into as many areas of social life as possible.

For the liberal, elections are valuable political instruments, but they are instruments towards liberal ends. We must draw a distinction between democracy — rule by popular will — and a liberal state that uses elections to appoint its executive and hold it to account. That is to say that elections are a means of organising the political life of a people that can, in cooperation with other institutions, ensure that liberal values are protected. Liberalism is primarily a theory about the proper extent of the power of the state, while democracy is primarily a means of deciding who should rule, and in whose interest.

One of the interesting features of the political development of the West was that the question of the proper extent of political power became a part of the debates about the proper political order of a society. From the sixteenth through to the nineteenth centuries the West's political thought concentrated on the nature of political power rather than on the personnel of government. Even when political actors made the case for or against the right of a certain individual or group to rule they did so with one eye on the nature of the political system as a whole. Perhaps the chief theme in British political thought throughout this period was the struggle between the people and the executive. The assertion that individuals have rights and that these rights limit the extent of what those in political authority can do to them is perhaps the most powerful conceptual theme in British political history and thinking.

Some Western countries such as Britain and the United States became liberal before, and in some cases long before, they became fully democratic. The struggle for liberty from the sixteenth century only gradually became a struggle for democracy in the nineteenth and twentieth centuries. Even the struggle for the extension of the franchise was a struggle for the liberal right of political representation rather than a fully fledged endorsement of democracy.

What are the main ingredients of Western success? The following brief analysis shows that they are liberal in nature, to do with *restricting* the power of government, and largely unconnected with the process of *electing* governments.

Individual Rights

One of the West's greatest achievements has been the development of the notion of individual rights: a set of moral and legal privileges that protect the individual from interference or coercion by others. The notion of rights has gradually evolved from ancient Rome, through the Middle Ages and Reformation, and into the modern world. It has acquired an increasingly sophisticated conceptual language that can be used to articulate a series of absolute proscriptions of behaviour. To say that an individual has a right to do something is to say that no other individual, or group of individuals, has a right to interfere in that action. This is very important in the development of the West. On one level legal enforcement of individual rights obviously reduces the scope for coercion in social life and provides a legalistic language that facilitates conflict resolution in disputes between individuals. But what is often overlooked is the contribution of rights to the very notion of individualism. By giving individuals a protected sphere of choice into which others have no right to stray we open the space for the flourishing and exploration of human individuality. The only status that becomes significant is one's status as an individual. Nobility or clerical office no longer provides a warrant to exercise authority not open to others.

The history of the West has been a long struggle against oppression and for the right of individuals to control their own lives. The gradual development of the language of individual rights and its percolation through our moral thinking and legal practice has created a culture where the use of power and coercion must be justified to each individual against whom it is attempted. While we might have some doubts about particular extensions of the terminology of rights it is nonetheless clear that the general notion has been one of the most liberating ideas in human history.

The Rule of Law

The legal institutions that grew with the idea of individual rights are another foundation stone of the West. The notion that law should rule rather than any particular individual is an ancient, Roman idea, but the success of the West has been to make this a reality for an extended period of time. The idea that human laws are a written version of a wider moral or natural law allowed the West to provide a freestanding set of rules that governed human social life. The authority of these rules was held to be such that they acted as a trump card against the claims or judgment of any particular individual. The belief in law as a universally binding set of principles meant that the West was gradually able to develop the idea that there were no exceptions to the legal order — that the law binds us all equally. The law found its expression differently in different legal traditions, but in all of them the idea that the law was articulated in general terms and applied universally took hold. Whether in the precedent of the common law tradition or the codes of the Roman tradition the law was seen as the framework of rules that made social life possible without arbitrary intervention from the powerful, and which bore the moral beliefs of the community.

Alongside this, Western countries gradually developed a series of institutions to decide and enforce the law. Chief among the characteristics of these institutions were the impartiality of judges and the jury system. Both of these practices had the effect of preventing the corruption of the legal process to serve the ends of those in positions of power. Trial by peers or before a legal bench committed to the law and not beholden to political authority changed the nature of the exercise of the West's system for resolving disputes among individuals.

The significance of the rule of law was further extended by the development of the notion of a basic political law.

The West came to believe that its political orders were the product of a body of constitutional law that laid down the terms of political association and the relationship of political institutions. Constitutionalism became one of the greatest forces for binding the activities of political actors that mankind has yet developed. The idea that the activities of a power-holder could be deemed 'unconstitutional' serves as a check on the exercise of political office.

Limited Government

One consequence of the idea of the rule of law was that the exercise of political authority became subject to rules. This marked the start of the limitation of the activities of governments. In earlier forms of human society the exercise of power was limited only by the extent to which that power was checked by other power holders. But with the gradual development of the Western legal order we increasingly came to see the identification of government as a specific and limited activity. Not only were those in power limited by the rule of law and the emerging legal order but they also became subject to a powerful set of culturally embedded views about what a government was for.

The clearest expression of this conceptual understanding of the limitations of government is to be found in the struggle to control executive power. How better to oppose what you view as an abuse of power than to depict it as an illegitimate action, as an extension of power beyond the bounds dictated by the social function of government? This way of thinking about politics developed into a tradition of limited government.

It was in the context of this limitation of the exercise of power that the discussion about the legitimacy of government was undertaken. The notion that legitimate political authority depended on the consent of the people was less important than the concept that authority had bounds, and that stepping over those bounds was a ground for removing consent. Notice here that the force of this argument depends as much on the liberal idea of restricting power — legitimate power is limited power — as it does on the idea of consent as a basis for legitimacy. This was reflected in the fact that liberal theories of resistance to tyranny depended on the withdrawal of consent after the abuse of power by those in authority. The restriction of arbitrary power through law and through the limitation of the exercise of coercion by political institutions greatly reduced the danger of the tyrannical abuse of power in the West.

Religious Toleration

Perhaps the greatest achievement of the West was the hard won, if often unintentional, achievement of a settlement that allowed those of different religious confessions to live side by side in the same political society. The religious schism of the Reformation led to centuries of bloodshed within and between the nations of the West. But eventually each of the Western nations came to some accommodation that allowed civil peace to be maintained. Religious toleration did not mean an end to religious differences, nor did it mean equality of status between religions, but it did mean that individuals accepted that they should not use violence to enforce their religious beliefs on others. The civil peace that this allowed saw a gradual extension of religious toleration in Western countries. Freedom to practise religion gradually became enshrined in the legal orders of the West in such a way as to preclude violent religious conflict. This product of an exhaustion from futile religious conflicts led to the powerful idea of the separation of church and state. Taken to its furthest extent in the United States, this involved the recognition that religious belief was a matter of individual conscience and as such it was inappropriate for the state to favour or enforce any particular religion.

Like many of the values of liberalism, religious toleration was not a product of a philosophical argument. Instead it was a gradually evolved set of practices that only came to be regarded as a value once its success had been demonstrated in practice.

Intellectual Freedom

Once the rule of law and individual rights became recognised and the danger of religious persecution had been set aside the West had created the space for intellectual freedom to develop. Once the use of force in defence of religious or intellectual orthodoxies had been constrained, individuals found themselves free to develop and discuss ideas and theories. The development of the empirical method in the sciences combined with this new era of freedom of speech and inquiry, led to the massive outpouring of learning that has characterised the last 300 years. Individual freedom and the confidence to express new or unpopular ideas allowed the creation of an international community of academics dedicated to the enhancement of human knowledge. The wealth generated by economic development allowed further specialisation and the modern academic disciplines gradually arose from a division of labour in intellectual endeavour. Intellectual freedom is a prerequisite for successful inquiry and innovation, and it is these that have driven the scientific and technological advances that have transformed life in the West.

One other significant manifestation of intellectual freedom that developed in the West was the extension of the idea of freedom of speech into the idea of the freedom of the press. While this contributed to the intellectual development discussed above, it also developed an important political function. Free criticism of office holders became an informal check on the activities of government and helped to safeguard the achievements of liberal civilisation.

Property Rights

Among the most important of the individual rights that have been developed in the West are those that secure an individual's claim to his property. This is a vital part of the creation of the protected sphere of individual autonomy that other individual rights have created. Coercive power in non-liberal societies was and is often used to seize the goods and even the labour or lives of others. The recognition of a right to individual bodily integrity was followed by recognition of a right to the product of one's labour. This is perhaps the most monumental achievement in Western civilisation — the creation of a legal order that recognises ownership and enforces it through a legal system. The gradual creation of a political and legal order that actively enforced private ownership and restricted the attempt to use status, authority or force to expropriate the goods of another led to a sea change in both economic and political life. In political life it meant that the state could, to a great extent, no longer be the source of private revenue which it had been in previous civilizations. In the economic realm it meant that individuals now had stable conditions of ownership. This meant that they were able to engage in productive activity without fear of the result being seized from them. This stability of expectations allowed the investment of effort and thought into improved production — the secret that lies behind the vast outpouring of wealth that the West has generated in the last 300 years.

Markets

If property rights and the rule of law paved the way for the economic success of the West they were only able to do so because of the development of a set of institutions and practices that we now refer to as the market economy. Security of property holding allowed individuals to concentrate on improving the productive output that they could create with their holdings. This, as Adam Smith famously observed, led to the gradual development of the division of labour which is the true source of the wealth of nations. Specialisation in production is only possible if there is the opportunity for mutually beneficial trade between specialists. Once individuals enjoyed a degree of stability in their property holdings they began to concentrate their labour on particular tasks and then meet to exchange goods in a market. This primitive form of production and exchange gradually developed into the complex economic interactions that characterise the modern Western economy.

Early liberals like Smith were among the first to realise the true nature and origins of wealth. They supported the pursuit of economic development, but they also saw that this humanitarian goal was best pursued by permitting the gradually evolved institutions of the market to encourage individuals to interact. Left on their own under the security of the rule of law, individuals make use of the information and capital available from markets to maximise their wealth. They do this by entering into mutually beneficial exchanges and thus serving the interests of others. The open and voluntary exchange that occurs in markets was the catalyst for the specialisation and division of labour that have driven wealth generation. That the inhabitants of the West enjoy unprecedented levels of material comfort is a direct result of the gradual evolution of market exchange and contracts under the rule of law.

Civil Society

One consequence of the rise of the rule of law and the development of limitations on the activities of government was that individuals were left free to form voluntary associations. The gradual evolution of a distinct realm of human association that we have come to call civil society has been characteristic of the West. These associations range from traditional universities and churches, to more modern mutual welfare organisations, charities and sports clubs. The existence of these voluntary associations provides a third form of human interaction that is neither the family nor the state. They demonstrate that individuals choose to associate without the need for coercion. Civil society represents an arena in which autonomous individuals can bond together with like-minded others in the pursuit of some shared practice or goal. This form of social interdependence marked a real development in human social life. It significantly reduced the extent to which individuals were dependent on the powerful within an established social hierarchy.

Social Freedom

One of the chief characteristics of Western countries is the high degree of social freedom that has developed over the last three centuries. Once individual rights came to be respected and individual conscience came to be accepted as the guide in matters of science, politics or religion, the precedent was set for alternative ways of living to flourish. Once the West had developed the idea that the power of the state should be constrained and that the individual was the base unit of moral value, then many of the other socially enforced norms gradually became separated from the state. More liberal attitudes to the arts, leisure pastimes, sexual relations and so on can be understood on one level as extensions of individual rights, but on another level they represent the recognition that the government has no role in enforcing particular visions of the good life. Many aspects of social morality have gradually moved into the private sphere in the West. This does not mean that there is agreement on these matters, but what it does mean is that it is no longer considered appropriate for the state to enforce a particular lifestyle upon the population as a whole.

The space created by this privatisation of morality has allowed an increasingly rich patchwork of ways of life to develop as individuals pursue happiness in the manner that suits them best. These expressions of individual autonomy only became possible when the state retreated from its traditional role as moral guardian.

Individualism

The sum result of all of the liberal developments above can be characterised as the achievement of individualism. Human life has moved on in the West from the conditions of bare survival in superstition-ridden tyrannies that have characterised most of human history. Our era is one of unprecedented freedom, security and material comfort. In the wake of this, and an integral part of its success, has been the development of a set of institutions and beliefs that value the individual human being. For the first time in human history large numbers of people are able to enjoy the economic and political security that allows them to explore their own individuality. In Western countries individuals now have the freedom and the opportunity to pursue their own understanding of what makes them happy and secure. They are free because the individuals and institutions that hold power have been limited in their ability to enforce their own preferences upon them. Indeed it may not be an exaggeration to say that human individuality did not really exist until the West stumbled upon the means of allowing it to flourish.

* * *

Democracy, or rather electoral accountability, does have its place in the list of the achievements of the West, but only if seen as one of a whole range of means by which the coercive power of government can be restricted. What elections did bring to the story was a means of providing for the peaceful transfer of political power. The orderly transfer of power on a regular basis provided a further check on the abuse of power in society. It also reduced the incidence of civil war and curbed the ability of elites to shape the political order to their own advantage, because they are subject to periodic removal by the electorate or their representatives.

But the defining feature of liberalism is that it has limited the use of coercive force in society. Most significantly it has restricted the use and abuse of power by those in political authority. Liberalism has championed the private over the public, the individual over the collective, and the ordinary person over the politician. The problem with democracy, as we will see, is that it reverses this process. Democrats like politics, they believe in the use of coercive power as a force for good in the world and they see the liberal barriers designed to protect the private concerns of the individual as an obstacle to the success of their political schemes.

The West owes its success to its belief in liberal values and the gradual historical evolution of institutions like the rule of law and concepts such as individual rights. This is not to pretend that at any stage there existed a liberal utopia. The establishment of liberal institutions in the West was everywhere gradual, hesitant and imperfectly applied. But they are nonetheless the distinctive features at the root of Western success. Democracy is a relative latecomer to this cultural achievement and in the rest of this volume we want to suggest that is of dubious value for the continued success of the West.

Chapter Two

Warnings from the Past

If men were angels, no government would be necessary. If angels were to govern men, neither external nor internal controls on government would be necessary (Madison et al. 1987, pp. 319–20).

One of the most striking features of twenty-first century political life in the West is the near universal belief that most of the basic political questions have been answered. No serious alternative to something that has become known as liberal democracy has been advanced for some time. When we talk of democracy today we are almost always referring to this mixture of liberal principles and democratic principles. But this obscures the complicated relationship between these two very different concepts. In everyday conversation democracy is held to be synonymous with the protection of individual rights, with constitutionalism and with the defence of liberty. Even a cursory glance will tell us that there might be important everyday cases where the will of a democratically elected government infringes individual rights and reduces liberty. That there may be times when we have to choose between the will of the majority and the needs, hopes and desires of individuals.

Like all forms of intellectual and moral complacency this certainty about liberal democracy is both misguided and dangerous. This is especially the case given the potential intellectual incoherence that lies at the very heart of the notion of a liberal democracy. What would be left of our

cherished ideal if we were to come to realise that liberalism
and democracy were fatally in tension, or that the pursuit of
one of these ideals inevitably undermined the other?

We should have been warned about the dangers that
democracy poses to liberalism. After all, we've been thinking about it for long enough. From the Greeks to the Mod-
erns the ideas of democracy and liberty have had an uneasy
co-existence. From Aristotle's rejection of democracy as the
worst form of government, to John Stuart Mill's fear of an
oppressive tyranny of the majority, it has never been universally accepted that democratic institutions would secure
liberty. This chapter surveys the exploration of this tension
between democracy and liberty in the work of some of the
greatest figures in the Western philosophical canon.

Before we begin we should pause to re-iterate the two
senses in which democracy is generally used. The most
obvious of these is democracy in relation to an electoral system. For the ancients democracy implied the direct participation of the people in political decision making. In our own
time it has come to refer to a right to participate in the election of representatives who take part in political decision
making. We might call this democracy as a means. The second sense in which democracy is commonly used is as a
substantive political ideal — as something which is a value
to be pursued rather than an institutional tool to be
deployed in the pursuit of some other end. This sense of
democracy, democracy as an end, involves some sort of
commitment to substantive egalitarian principles. A society
is more democratic to the extent that it is characterised by
greater levels of equality between its members. Both of these
senses of the term are relevant to our present discussion.

*   *   *

Since the beginning of political philosophy serious doubts
have been raised about the desirability of democracy. In *The
Republic*, written in the 5th Century BC, Plato famously worried that the people lacked the rational capacity, education
and skill to make effective political decisions. Government

was a job for experts who would govern in the interest of the community. But he revised the idealism of this model in *The Laws* by recognising that the best practicable government is one where the rule of law prevails and the contingencies of individual character are replaced by certain regulations.

A generation later Aristotle reaches a similar conclusion in *The Politics*. Here democracy is characterised as the rule of the many (or poor) in the interest of the many (or poor). This is a corrupted form of government for Aristotle because the end of policy is a sectional interest and not the interest of the community at large. For Aristotle a balanced, constitutionally limited form of government (polity) is the best practicable form of political association. This form of government creates conditions of political stability while being the most likely to produce outcomes in the interest of the whole community.

For both Plato and Aristotle the analysis of ancient democracy suggests that it tends towards tyranny. They trace the rise of demagogues becoming tyrants through the manipulation of the grievances of the masses. The idea here is that democracy is unstable and that it tends to sectarian rule in such a way that it may be exploited by the unscrupulous yet politically gifted. Allied to this criticism is an examination of one of its most likely manifestations — the redistribution of wealth from a minority (rich) to the majority (poor). While this supposed tendency to despotism was partly a contingent feature of ancient city states it nonetheless points us towards a deeper, more structural problem of systems of government that draw legitimacy from majoritarianism. They 'tend' to create a specific set of incentives for the individuals who live in them. That is to say, they create an incentive to seek power by acting in the interests of the majority rather than of the community as a whole.

The ancient Greek concern about democracy and support for mixed forms of constitution was mirrored in the Roman world. Here again, in the writing of thinkers such as the orator Cicero and the historian Polybius, law and constitutions became key instruments for restraining the excesses of democracy. It is with Cicero and the notion of *res publica* (the public matters) that we begin also to see a more detailed consideration of the proper scope of political activity. Politics was considered as having a proper, defined, subject matter and political institutions were understood as being directed towards that subject matter.

While the kinds of society that the ancient Greeks and Romans inhabited are very different from our own, their ruminations on democracy have cast a long shadow on Western thought. Perhaps their greatest influence lies in the notion that the best practicable form of government is one that mixes different forms of rule under a constitution or set of basic laws. This idea of a balanced constitution dominated British thought from the seventeenth century. The notion was that the potential dangers of each form of government — monarchy, aristocracy and democracy — could be constrained by a series of institutional limitations and balances that were fixed in the constitutional structure of the polity.

In the eighteenth century foreign admiration of the British constitutional settlement was effusive. The French philosopher Montesquieu, in his *Spirit of the Laws*, published in 1748, praised the British constitution as the best yet developed for the defence of liberty. His admiration for the British model stemmed from the fact that it was the only nation 'whose constitution has political liberty for its direct purpose' (1989, p. 156). Liberty was secured because the potential for tyranny by any one group in society was checked by the balanced mixture of institutions suspended in a constitutional order. For example, the abuse of power in the name of the majority was precluded by placing restrictions on the majority's ability to exercise its will.

Montesquieu defines three possible forms of government as: 'republican government is that in which the people as a body, or only a part of the people, have sovereign power; monarchical government is that in which one alone governs, but by fixed and established laws; whereas, in despotic government, one alone, without law and without rule, draws everything along by his will and his caprices' (1989, p. 10). In this he was expressing the widespread fear that excessive power in the hands of the executive branch of government would result in despotism. The extent and nature of political power becomes a separate question from that of who shall hold that power. The liberal contrast being set up is between government constrained by the rule of law and arbitrary power exercised by despots. This contrast reveals a new attitude towards politics. It is understood as a specific and limited activity and one which, if it oversteps its bounds, becomes despotic.

For the liberal the central political question becomes one of avoiding the danger of despotism. In Montesquieu's view democracy proved to be an unsatisfactory route to avoiding despotism. He believed that the lesson of the English Civil War was that democracy and liberty were not necessarily related. Indeed the search for liberty in democracy led instead to tyranny. This was a result of the dismantling of the checks and balances that kept the democratic element of the constitution in place. By removing constraints that acted to limit the political power of the sovereign the English discovered that even a 'democratic' sovereign could soon become a tyrannical protectorate operating in the name of the people. Montesquieu's historical study led him to the liberal conclusion that democracy without limitations, without checks and balances, would tend towards despotism. It would destroy what it was intended to protect.

Montesquieu and the British Whigs proved to be deeply influential in their concerns about democracy and their preference for a mixed and constitutionally limited form of government. This influence often took the form of a particular animus against the executive branch of government. eighteenth century political discourse is awash with the fear of the corruption of the executive. While most of these thinkers accepted the need for an executive function in government, and supported the idea of suspending this power in a constitutional set of checks and balances, they also worried that this exercise of political power through executive office was, by its nature, corruptive of the political order. The fear was that the executive would be in a position to assert its will over other elements in a constitutional balance. Through its control of increasing revenue from Britain's colonies, the executive could manage the political system through patronage. The eighteenth century political writer Viscount Bolingbroke observed that the executive sought to 'buy the votes of the people with the money of the people' (1997, p. 53). The main ways of doing this were to provide government pensions and to rig elections in rotten boroughs by bribing or blackmailing voters. Richard Price, the early liberal philosopher, feared that Parliament had 'degenerated into a body of sycophants' (1991, p. 42) willing to follow the whims of the executive in return for place and wealth.

Even at this early stage, before anything like a full system of electoral democracy was in place, we see the main themes that illustrate the tension between liberalism and democracy begin to emerge. If the executive is in some notional sense checked by a democratic assembly, there are means for the balance to be unsettled and these means lie at the disposal of the executive.

Nowhere was this accusation of corruption more loudly heard than in Britain's North American colonies. The political philosophers of the American Revolution identified corruption as a major danger to be guarded against in their new political system. They also wanted to have liberty as the central value of their new nation. To achieve these ends they turned to the Whig ideas of constitutionalism and mixed government. The *Federalist Papers* are one of the most detailed and significant extended discussions of the relationship between liberty and democracy. Throughout his contribution James Madison worries about the danger of an 'elective despotism' (1987, p. 310) that would come from a failure to separate the powers of government. For Madison it is 'the very definition of tyranny' (*Ibid.*, p. 303) to place the powers of government in a single set of hands — however democratically selected those might be. The result of this is the now familiar notion of a constitution that defines both the structure of government and the limits to be placed on the extent of that government's legitimate sphere of activity.

Again the fear is that democracy would prove to be unstable and would lead to the sacrifice of the rights of the individual to the interests of the majority. Madison's desire to underline the point that the proposed system of American government was to be republican and not democratic is well known. Though he did not yet use the term 'liberalism' to describe his position it seems fair to place him in the tradition of those for whom the case for liberty outweighed the attraction of democracy.

But Madison has a further contribution to make to our survey of doubts about democracy. Without a constitutional order we would see a politics of factional interaction where political authority was exchanged between the adherents of particular groups who wished to capture the authority of the state for their own interests. Under this system the value of democracy is chiefly that it allows for the peaceful transfer of power from one elite to another. This, perhaps, should not be sniffed at too haughtily. Changes in power can occur in a far more destabilising manner and it would certainly be a mark of the usefulness of democracy if it minimises political violence. However, as the philosopher Anthony De Jasay has recently pointed out, to attribute peaceful changes of government to democracy is a mistake. What actually does the work in the peaceful change of regimes is not so much the democratic mandate as the respect for the constitutional rules that determine the process of changing government. There is no essential reason why this process need be democratic. Indeed, historically, the peaceful change of government in liberal states like Britain preceded the extension of the franchise and the popular recognition of the value of democratic sovereignty. In fact, a change of government in Britain still does not require an election, though control of Parliament was (and is) usually necessary.

* * *

It is the influence of the eighteenth century Genevan philosopher Jean-Jacques Rousseau that gave renewed impetus to the concept of democracy as a legitimate form of government in itself. In his *Social Contract* Rousseau argued that it would be possible to create a democratic system that would ensure that, by participating in decision making directly, we would control the power of the state and ensure that it was directed at the common good. This misapprehension is largely responsible for our current confusion over the relative value of democracy and liberty. Its roots lie in a failure to distinguish between a legitimate government and the legitimate extent of the activities of government.

The modern philosophical interest in democracy is largely coloured by the republican thinking of Rousseau. Rousseau's influence extends from Immanuel Kant and Karl Marx down to contemporary exponents of 'deliberative democracy'. The ancient idea of a democratic community of equals participating in a direct democracy is transformed in Rousseau's hands into a polity where the democratic nature of the decision making procedure legitimises its outcomes. At the same time the pursuit of the ideal of democracy provides the principle of government. The identification and pursuit of the 'general will' lies at the heart of this understanding of politics. Rousseau believed that this will was an expression of what was in the interest of the community as a whole and, crucially, that this was distinct from the aggregate of the interests of its individual members. Decisions directed by the general will are always legitimate for Rousseau. That is to say that we might be misguided in identifying the nature of the general will and what policies it implies, but that the will itself remains in existence waiting to be found and thus always rightful. To his credit he recognises that the system he advocates is republican rather than purely democratic, but the damage had been done with the notion that the locus of legitimacy lies in submission to the will of the community. For this immediately raises the question: 'How do we determine this will?' Leading to the answer: 'through democracy'.

In Rousseau's thought we enter a 'social contract' where individuals undertake: 'the complete alienation by each associate member to the community of all his rights' (1960,

p. 180). For Rousseau we are freed from our selfish and animalistic instincts when we submit ourselves to the rational direction of our activity as a member of a political community. I cease to consider myself as an individual alone and now, in my every political decision, view myself as a member of a community, and the interest of the community as the aim of my activity. This understanding of democracy lionises politics as the ultimate expression of human communal life. Politics becomes a noble enterprise to be pursued rather than a necessity to be put up with.

The result of this line of thought is the idea that an original social contract, leading to a democratic institutional framework where individuals guide their decisions towards the interest of the community as a whole, is the proper nature of political association. This has had a profound impact on political philosophy.

The problem for Rousseau is that people might disagree about the general will or about how it ought to be implemented, and the only answer left to this is that, if each is thinking about the general will then a democratic procedure will be an effective means of identifying what that will is. While he seeks to downplay this element of his thought it becomes troubling when we consider that he also regards the social contract as the basis for the legitimate exercise of coercion in society. The social compact legitimises the exercise of coercive force: 'whoever shall refuse to obey the general will must be constrained by the whole body of his fellow citizens to do so: which is no more than to say that it may be necessary to compel a man to be free—freedom being that condition which, by giving each citizen to his country, guarantees him from all personal dependence' (*Ibid.*, p. 184).

What is worrying about Rousseau's thought is that it combines three elements with distinctly illiberal tendencies. First, the notion that individual freedom has its realisation only in submission to communal life. Rousseau no doubt hoped to capture the idea of the community as defender of the rights of individuals, but he has expressed it in such a way that community is the locus of value rather than the individual. Second, Rousseau believed that this need not be a problem because he is referring only to democratic communities directed towards the general will. Thus the application of coercion will be guided by the interest of the community which will in turn subsume the real interest of the individual. Third, an individual who does not submit to the institutional structures of this system can legitimately be coerced into doing so as the democratic nature of the community and its decision process warrant obedience. Moreover because life as a citizen is the ultimate realisation of human freedom we have a moral as well as a political responsibility to obey.

It is from Rousseau onwards that we start to see the ideas of democracy and liberalism depart from each other. A democratic mandate in the pursuit of democratic ideals provides a moral trump against the protection of liberal rights. What is decided by democratic means and is in the pursuit of democratic goals overrides concerns about its effect on individuals. In the nineteenth century liberals such as John Stuart Mill and Alexis de Tocqueville contested this point by describing the danger of a 'tyranny of the majority'. From here we see the continued development of a line of thought that stresses the difference between liberalism and democracy. Liberalism wishes to protect the liberty of the individual by placing constraints, often in the form of individual rights, upon the activities of any government. This led to the view that democracy was of value largely as a means to the end of protecting liberal values. For Mill democratic elections developed as a part of the liberal checks on the power of government. They ceased to be of value for this end if they were taken as warranting the infringement of individual rights.

In the nineteenth and twentieth centuries the movement for the extension of the franchise — the liberal right to political representation — became dangerously confused with the notion that the democratic will of the people provided a source of political legitimacy that overwhelmed all others. The introduction of universally enfranchised democracies changed the nature of the West. It led to the creation of a new form of political conduct. This form of conduct gradually abandoned the liberal view that there are suitable constraints on the scope of government activity and replaced it with the notion that the limits of government activity are determined by the views of the majority. Whatever the majority believes ought to be law can be legitimately enforced as such. As we will see in the next chapter this has led to the gradual erosion of the notion of individual rights. Rousseau is triumphant.

* * *

The American authors of the *Federalist Papers* believed that government, through constitutionally limited and balanced representative assemblies, would maintain a close dependency between those in power and those whom they were supposed to represent. The problem with this belief was that it proved to be anything but the case. From the 1950's onwards a new set of conceptual tools were developed to understand the structure and practice of modern mass democracy. Growing from the work of political economists such as Anthony Downs, James Buchanan and Gordon Tullock, the notion of using economic incentive structures to understand the behaviour of political actors became a key part of political science. The lessons of this approach are that the behaviour of political representatives is directed by the desire to retain office and that this powerfully affects their activity. As these 'public choice' scholars showed so clearly, representatives became subject to a set of incentives that encouraged them to innovate in order to gain the support of the voters.

The importance of this observation is that the structure of modern democratic communities comes nowhere near the model hoped for by Rousseau and his followers. Instead a modern democracy functions by the assembly of majority coalitions of voters behind a particular set of representatives. These representatives are then given access to the executive powers of the state which they can use to reward the interests of those who have brought them to power. In one sense this is precisely what the eighteenth century liberals feared, but their notion of corruption is insufficient to explain this process. What we see instead is something far closer to Plato and Aristotle's concern. The distribution of the benefits and burdens of society becomes an object of political manipulation. A shifting set of majorities coalesces around particular representatives and is then used to maintain that elite in power.

For the public choice scholars this process is crystallised in the notion of 'concentrated benefits and diffused costs'. This simple principle shows how an executive can use the taxation system to extract a small amount from each member of the population — sometimes so small that the individual has no objection to it. However, when each of these small contributions is brought together into a larger stock they can be channelled towards a particular section of society. The provision of such asymmetric advantages allows the executive to manage the interest groups that it needs to form its majority coalition.

This process has been greatly compounded by the shift in opinion about the function of government that accompanied the rise of democratic socialism. The belief that the government had a duty to secure the welfare of the people meant that the size of the state and the scope of its activities were vastly increased in the twentieth century. This commitment to state re-distribution as a core feature of the political order of mass democracy further eroded the notion that liberty must be protected by placing strict limitations on the activities of the state. Such re-distribution is not regarded as direct petty corruption but rather 'right' as in the service of the egalitarian ideal of democracy. Which is to say that the democratic nature of the electoral system and the pursuit of the ideal of democracy in distributive justice lead to a belief that it is precisely the function of government to redistribute the benefits and burdens of society to democratic ends. The idea of social justice as a legitimate function of state activity allows the development of a new set of relationships between the elected officials and the groups that benefit from their largesse. All of this is licensed by the intellectual confusion of liberty and democracy.

One may well think that the contemporary interest in human rights laws might limit the activities of government and retain at least some element of the eighteenth century concern for the rights of the individual. And to a certain extent this is the case, but the creation of so-called 'positive rights', rights whose satisfaction demands redistributive intervention by the state, such as a right to a minimum income or a right to health care, has actually resulted in a further extension of the activities of the democratic state. The perception that it is the duty of the government to bring about the conditions desired under a regime of 'rights' was perfectly liberal when those rights were restricted to liberal rights of forbearance, but when the language of rights was extended into the so-called social rights this quickly compounded the pressure on the state to serve the interests of the people through re-distribution. This, of course, warrants further government activity in the name of what is 'right'.

* * *

In recent years many political philosophers like Jürgen Habermas and John Rawls have adopted a further position that blends both of the senses of democracy that we identified at the start of this chapter. The distinction between the liberal, who sees democracy as a strictly limited means to restrict the abuse of power, and the committed democrat who sees democracy as legitimising the pursuit of egalitarian social policy, is absent in the work of these thinkers. Their concern is with democracy as a deliberative process characteristic of the 'Public Sphere'. This understanding, drawing on the work of Rousseau and the French philosopher Condorcet, sees democratic debate as both legitimising in a political sense, but also valuable in an epistemic, or knowledge gathering, sense. The concern here is with creating a democratic speech environment. A forum where individuals are able to participate on an equal footing in a discussion of the values that ought to direct their community. The focus is not on majoritarianism as a decision principle, but rather on consensus achieved through rational deliberation. This procedural deliberation is held to be of value both because it embodies core egalitarian values and because it provides an arena for debate and persuasion that, so it is argued, will be more likely to result in considered decisions that are genuinely in the interest of the whole of the community. Such an ideal situation would then result in decisions that could be considered to be the general will of the whole community.

It will be immediately apparent that this is, at least on one level, simply a re-iteration of Rousseau. As such it falls prey to some of the objections that we raised earlier. The overwhelming stress on democracy means that the clause demanding consensus is the only real check against the abuse of individual rights by a majority. This, of course, is precisely where the deliberative democrats hit a problem. In their idealised model, as in Rousseau's idealised model, consensus is plausible and appears to be a sufficient check on the abuse of minorities. But of course this is highly unrealistic in anything like non-ideal situations. Indeed it is tantamount to solving the problem of the tyranny of a majority over a minority by assuming that minorities do not exist or that they will be persuaded to acquiesce to the will of the majority. Rousseau admitted this as we saw. But the deliberative democrats, with their focus on democracy's epistemic role rather than its function as a check on the exercise of political power, often either fail to see this or regard it as irrelevant to their abstract position. The position that they approach seems to be something like this. That society is more desirable the closer its institutions approach to the practices of deliberative democracy. Both legitimacy and a greater likelihood of making 'correct' decisions are then likely. Pursuit of the ideal of democracy thus serves as a directional guidance for the polity and institutions that serve as a structural barrier to it are to be opposed.

*   *   *

In the classical liberal tradition democracy has always been regarded as a means rather than an end. Democracy is not the prime political value upon which this liberalism based its claims. Instead it was just one of many institutional means that were developed to protect the core ideal of individual liberty. Democracy was desirable to the extent that it acted as a limitation and constraint on the activities of the executive. A degree of accountability and responsibility could be enshrined through competitive elections.

Similarly the liberal commitment to equal liberty for all was partly realised in the extension of the franchise and this in turn acted as the embodiment of the ideal of the equal value of each individual. But liberals were always clear that there was a limit to the usefulness, and hence the desirability, of democracy. Taken to extremes democracy becomes little more than might (in terms of numbers) declared right. This was fundamentally illiberal. Further this illiberality can be traced through the idea that the generation of a democratic mandate legitimises any action of the state. No liberal could countenance this as it would place the rights of the individual in a precarious position subject to the whims of shifting majority opinion.

For liberals like Mill the danger was not simply that of a tyranny of the majority in the sense of it using the political system to extort advantages for its members. It was more than this — it was the very idea that the individual could be asked to submit to the will of the majority even when that majority was activated by a desire to act in the individual's interest. The fear of paternalism, of a democratically elected majority using the coercive power of the state to pursue the majority's vision of what is good for individuals, lies at the heart of Mill's liberalism.

Without a protected sphere of individual activity, a sphere into which no government, not even one in command of a democratic mandate, could trespass, Mill thought there was little hope for human liberty. For Mill this meant that the development of the individual as a responsible moral agent would be fatally undermined. The exercise of freedom in making decisions about individual well being was both epistemically and morally necessary for Mill.

It is here that we see the real tension between those that stress democracy as a value and those that stress liberty as a value. For those in favour of liberty there are certain things that the state ought not to do. There is a certain area of human activity that, regardless of the views of other individuals in however significant a majority, ought to be protected. For the committed democrat the interest of 'the people' should direct the state and that interest is identified by what the majority (or its leaders) think it entails. As the Austrian philosopher F.A. Hayek noted: 'The tragic illusion was that the adoption of democratic procedures made it possible to dispense with all other limitations on governmental power' (1982, p. 3).

This has proved to be a dangerous intellectual error. But it has become all the more dangerous given the growth of the idea that political activity is an expression of the noblest features of human life and character. When allied with a substantively egalitarian ideal of democracy this attitude sees politics as a practice to be celebrated and developed rather than feared and restricted. So we regard as legitimate a state not so different from the tyrannies of the past.

Chapter Three

Democracy and the Abuse of Law

As we noted in the previous chapters, the historical development and philosophical consideration of liberty and democracy has been more complicated than might be supposed. The simplest way to grasp this point is to understand that politics is about the use of coercive power. More importantly it is the exercise of sovereign coercive power — power that claims a monopoly in a geographic territory. Two central questions quickly arise in any consideration of politics. 'Who is to have power?' and 'What is the proper extent of this power?' Democracy is predominantly a way of answering the first question while liberalism has always been an attempt to answer the second.

The classical liberals thought that they had found an answer to their fears that democracy would dissolve into a tyranny of the majority. The answer, they thought, lay in the creation of a constitutional framework of checks and balances. By diffusing power, by dividing it between opposing arms of government, they thought that they would place sufficient barriers in the path of a majority to protect minorities. These institutions are familiar to us all — bi-cameral legislatures, federal layers of government, jury trials, an independent judiciary and civil service. However the checks and balances that they provided have proved only partially successful. They may have acted as a brake on the tendency of democratically elected politicians to bend the political system to their own interest, but the democratic process has gone ahead nonetheless.

One of the chief reasons for this has been the ability of activist politicians to provide plausible (and for that matter tenuous) re-interpretations of the particular verbal formulation of certain clauses of the various constitutional documents. The gradual extension of state activity in the United States in particular has been accompanied by an increasingly creative use of word twisting to provide ways around the strictures of the constitution.

Perhaps the clearest liberal attempt to limit the exercise of the will of the majority was the institution of formal Bills of Rights designed to protect individuals by delineating absolute restrictions on the actions of the state. These individual rights helped to secure a distinct private sphere that was to be free from interference by other individuals and the state. Quite simply, there were supposed to be things that no individual or combination of individuals was allowed to do to another individual. Not the least of the institutions that formed this protected sphere was the right to property. In the political discourse of the seventeenth and eighteenth century it was protection of property that formed the backdrop of the struggle for liberty. Now property in this understanding was not exclusively restricted to material possessions. It extended outwards from self-ownership of one's body, labour and political vote.

The institution of private property proved a vital brake on the power of the state. By dividing economic resources among the people of a society and securing them to their individual holders, Western societies effectively diffused economic power and thus reduced its availability as a tool of political coercion. As market exchange and economic development gradually raised living standards for greater numbers the power that comes with wealth gradually dispersed through society. The countries of the West moved from societies where political obedience was secured through material dependence within a rigid hierarchy to more fluid forms of social life.

This chapter describes how the misuse of law under democracy is undermining these institutional elements that protect the individual, in a process that is ultimately self-defeating.

* * *

One of the problems with constraining the abuse of the power of government through checks and balances was that some form of executive power was necessary for the smooth operation of political society. In other words there must be someone to take the initiative in defending the country and enforcing the law as defined by the legislature and judiciary. Liberals argued that this branch of government must be carefully balanced and checked — its functions restricted in such a way as to prevent abuse. The fear was that the executive, as the centre of the exercise of coercive power, would be in a position to dominate the political order. This worry, as we saw above, often took the form that the executive could bribe the electorate and offer position and wealth to those who acted in its interest. With the growth of the state in the twentieth century the scope for these abuses was greatly increased. As the state expanded, and the number of state agencies and quasi-state bodies grew, the scope for rewarding loyalty from the public purse expanded exponentially.

But as we noted above this rather obvious form of corruption was not the real worry that lay behind many of the liberal objections to democratic institutions. The real worry was that the state would be captured by a majority who regarded their numerical superiority as a warrant to impose their vision of how individuals ought to live on the rest of society. The danger would prove even more troubling than first appearances might suggest.

In the historical evolution of our current political order we saw the emergence of three distinct functions of government. The branches of government that the American Founders sought to divide with checks and balances were those identified by John Locke and others: executive, judicial, legislative. For early liberal thinkers like David Hume the institution of government arose historically in such a way that these functions were intertwined and often in the hands of a single person. Hume provides us with a conjectural history of the early development of government. During times of war members of a social group looked to particular individuals to lead them in combat. Later, during times of peace, this war leader became a respected figure who was called upon to judge in disputes between the members of the society. From this point on the chief became a judge and subsequently the lawgiver for primitive societies. For eighteenth century liberals tyranny was the location of all of these activities in the same hands. From our point of view what is of interest is that there are three distinct activities conducted by a government — the activity of legislation, the activity of judgment and the activity of the execution of policy. It is this distinction that will lie at the heart of this chapter — the distinction between law (understood as legislation and judgment) and policy as pursued by the executive.

The distinction is essential because in the last century modern democracy has seen the conflation of these three distinct elements once again. Understanding this process is central to our case that democracy is leading to the re-establishment of tyrannical government. Maintaining a clear separation between general rules embodying justice on one hand, and the pursuit of material improvement on the other has been an abiding theme of twentieth century liberal and conservative thinkers such as Hayek and Michael Oakeshott. This preoccupation is largely a result of a shift in the understanding of the nature of politics that occurred from the late nineteenth century onwards. Across Europe democratic socialist campaigners, especially groups like the Fabian Society, came to the view that the state and political power should be used as an engine for social change. This pragmatic adoption of state power to pursue desired social goals was both understandable and deeply worrying. The belief was that the moral goals behind the social democratic position were so pressing that the state would have to be entrusted with sufficient power to bring them into being. This would not lead to the sort of tyranny feared by the liberals because the power of the state would be constrained and directed by the democratic process. A shift in focus emerged — the question of the proper limits of state activity took a back seat to the seemingly more pressing issue of what powers the state would have to wield to bring about its desired goals. The role of the state changed fundamentally from maintaining the rule of law to engineering social change and development.

With this change we see a subtle transformation in the meaning of democracy. Democracy now becomes the rule of the people in the interests of the people in a moralised sense. Not only is it legitimised by the procedure of democratic election, but it is also legitimised by the end to which it is directed — the service of the people. From here it is a very short step to the position that we traced to Rousseau. That is, that the political power of the community is to be directed towards the good of the people and that the people's genuine democratic participation would make them willing to assent to what was necessary in pursuit of this general good. Those who dissented were in some sense acting against their own best interests as a member of the community and so might be coerced into accepting the decisions of the majority.

To oppose the will of the democratic majority under these conditions becomes not merely an expression of doubt about the danger of tyranny of the majority or an expression of individual dissent. It becomes an objection to the moral goal of democracy. You become at once a bad citizen and a bad person. The democratic state now concerns itself with the pursuit of substantive policy goals drawn from and justified by a notion of the public good. It is the job of the state not merely to facilitate the conditions of individual association and activity, but also to pursue the achievement of a set of goals that will improve not just the lives of citizens, but which will improve the citizens themselves. Under this understanding of the function of government we have seen a series of initiatives, policies, institutional changes and campaigns designed to alter the behaviour of citizens in a direction regarded as socially and individually beneficial by activist politicians secured of a democratic mandate. To pursue the good of the public is the qualifier of a good person and to mean well legitimises the use of coercive power to bring about desirable outcomes.

Such an approach should be very familiar to any observer of the activities of government in the modern democratic West. It also underpins more extreme versions of democratic socialism such as Marxism and Communism. Examples of this way of thinking are especially prominent in campaigns and initiatives to improve public health. Campaigns to persuade individuals to change their behaviour have given way to the use of incentives to encourage changes in behaviour and, at the extreme, to the use of the criminal law to make people act in a manner that is 'good for them'. This attitude is not restricted to the traditional left, but is pervasive across the political spectrum. The latest expression of this tendency is to be found in the 'nudge' phenomenon associated with supposedly libertarian paternalists such as Cass Sunstein. Here the notion is that individuals should be gently prompted towards behaviour that is 'good' for them through incentives. The role of the state is to direct its citizens towards what is good for them regardless, or even in spite of, their own inclinations. The notion behind this is the old idea that the vast majority of the people do not know what is good for them. What is curious about the current appearance of this Platonic theme is that it is now integrally related to democracy. What is good for the people is determined through a democratic process (as the epistemic democrats we noted above would argue) and when this process is complete there remains little ground for opposition. The elected politicians are there to represent the interests of the public regardless of what the public feels about it.

One worrying further development has been the decline in the notion of distinct public and private spheres. While there has been much handwringing about the decline of the public sphere illustrated by declining rates of political participation, significantly less concern has been devoted to the extension of the realm of politics into the areas of life previously regarded as private. One of the clearest manifestations of this was the feminist slogan 'The Personal is Political'. The slogan is designed to point to the different power relations in family units and the potential abuse and manipulation that lay there. But the laudable attempt to highlight domestic violence was very quickly extended into the idea that all interpersonal relationships and all human activity is deeply political and embodies power relationships — it is thus already political and so must be submitted to the same standards of political control and direction as exist in the society at large. Thus the state is warranted in regulating and interfering in virtually every aspect of the lives of its citizens. Nothing must be beyond the reach of the democratic state in a society that is political in all of its aspects. If the ideal that directs politics in this situation is an ideal of democracy then the democratic state is warranted in pursuing this goal by directing its citizens towards behaviour that more fully embodies democratic ideals.

This enormous growth in the power and activity of the state was regarded as legitimate because the system was democratic and so legitimate, and because, in the service of democratic ideals, the state had to have the power to act in the interest of the people. Well-meaning people with good intentions who are committed to the ideal of democracy are now willing to see their fellow citizens coerced into doing what they think is 'good' for them to an extent that would have been unimaginabe 100 years ago. All of this becomes deeply worrying for the liberal when we remember where we started. Politics is about the appropriate extent of the use of coercion in society. Democracy, which the liberals saw as part of the means to limiting the abuse of power, has become the legitimising principle of a massive extension of the use of coercion in society.

In practice the modern democratic polity inevitably falls significantly short of the idealised models of direct and deliberative democracy that preoccupy political philosophers. The reality of modern democracy is the world of professional politicians representing the electorate in the parliaments and assemblies that direct the political life of the nation. The nature of modern democracy has created a

class of career politicians whose job it is to legislate and
direct the political power of the state. Most of these politicians may be actuated by a desire to serve the public interest. They possess a vision of what is good for society and its
citizens and they want to use the political system to pursue
these goals. Regardless of party affiliation or the content of
these beliefs, the activity of the modern politician is remark-
ably similar. He aims to secure a position in his party, to
stand for and secure a winnable seat, to enter parliament
and to pursue the reforms that he thinks are in the public
interest.

Two sets of incentives are in operation here which tend
towards the creation of activist politicians. The first of these
is the moral incentive to do the right thing and to pursue
progressive outcomes through the institutions of the state.
It is this moral impetus that attracts people to politics and
which, while laudable, is open to the liberal doubt that it is
any business of politicians to make people do what they
think is good for them. The second set of incentives arises
within the democratic system itself. In order to get elected
and to remain in office the politician must show what he has
done for his constituents. This places a constant pressure on
the politician to act or to create the perception of activity. At
the level of government this takes the form of the sort of
coalition building that we noted in the previous chapter, but
it also leads to a near constant frenzy of activity. The result is
a constant stream of legislation and initiatives produced
and publicised as improving the lives of the citizens. No day
goes by without some sort of initiative or publicity campaign being introduced by one politician or another. The
widening public perception that it is the state's job to solve
the problems of society and its members provides the incentive of potential publicity that invites politicians to propose
government action.

Inevitably this frenzy of action often produces ill-thought
through or populist measures, but more significantly from
our point of view it also leads to a constant growth in the
size of the state and a constantly widening political realm.
The coercive apparatus of politics invades more and more

of our lives in the name of our own good. There is of course the further concern that once the government has acted to regulate a particular activity or has set in place a state apparatus to achieve particular goals it becomes next to impossible to step back from the intervention. Not only is there a public expectation that the state must act in this field because it has done so in the past, but there is now an interest group of civil servants with a specific interest in continuing and expanding government activity in that field. Professional politicians and interested bureaucrats react to the incentives provided by lobbyists and pressure groups to push a relentless growth in government activity. When, in living memory, has there been a significant process of repealing legislation?

* * *

From a liberal point of view these developments are worrying enough. But there is worse to come. The tendency to confuse law and policy has robbed the liberals of their main weapon against the potential excesses of the state. Previously we identified three functions of state activity: the function of making law, the function of judgment and the function of pursuing policy. These are conceptually distinct endeavours. Lawmaking aims at the expression of the general rules of conduct that ought to hold in the relationships between individual citizens and between the citizens and the state. Judgment involves the application of these general rules to particular cases. Policy, on the other hand, is the creature of the executive. It is directed towards the attainment of some specific desired set of circumstances. All of these activities are legitimate functions of the state. They are part of what we want and need politics to do for us. But the conceptual distinction between them is particularly important for liberals as it marks a boundary between two distinct areas of social life.

The confusion of these two types of activity (the making and judicial interpretation of laws, and the pursuit of policy) has been invited by the failure adequately to preserve a boundary between them in our political systems. Even where a nominal divide between executive and legislature is maintained the tendency has been for the executive to seek to influence and direct legislation. Over time this has led us to a situation where law is now regarded as a legitimate tool of social policy. It has increasingly become the case that the policy desires of a democratically elected government are taking the form of law and regulation as well as the provision of services. The confusion of these two conceptually distinct endeavours leads to a situation where it becomes acceptable to outlaw or regulate forms of activity in the pursuit of goals of social policy. This is seen as legitimate, of course, because the government enacting it is democratically elected and pursuing the interests of the public.

The result of this has been an explosion in the amount of legislation and regulation produced by our legislatures under the direction of the executive. In the name of the public good, of health and safety, of the environment and a host of other well-meant ideals, the activity of each citizen has been increasingly bound by rules designed to achieve public happiness. The danger of this for liberty should be immediately apparent. The boundary that defined the things that politics should be kept out of has been dangerously breached. Almost no element of human life is now immune from the political, from law designed to bring about desired policy goals and, as a result, from the exercise of coercion.

This situation is typified in the notion that regulations governing forms of behaviour can be introduced. As long ago as the eighteenth century the Scottish philosopher Adam Ferguson noted:

> Even with the best intentions towards mankind, we are inclined to think that their welfare depends, not on the felicity of their own inclinations, or the happy employment of their own talents, but on their ready compliance with what we have devised for their good (p. 250).

Ferguson observed that without the checks and balances of a liberal constitution we face the potential danger that government will devolve into a tyranny in the pursuit of the public good. The focus on the legitimising power of a democratic majority has led to the development of what we might call a 'ban' culture of paternalism. Politicians claim a right to regulate increasing areas of individual behaviour in the name of the democratic majority acting in the public interest.

The result is a greatly expanded role for government in almost every aspect of life and a consequence of this is that people look increasingly to the political process as a source of potential opportunities and largesse. The liberal philosophers had, of course, foreseen such a potential danger. Mill argued that the

> most cogent reason for restricting the interference of government, is the great evil of adding unnecessarily to its power. Every function superadded to those already exercised by the government, causes its influence over hopes and fears to be more widely diffused, and converts, more and more, the active and ambitious part of the public into hangers-on of the government, or of some party that aims to become the government (1991, p. 122).

The practical implications of this are explored in Chapter Four. It is unclear whether this sort of political moralising would have been able to become so prominent and so unobjected to an aspect of social life if it were not for the air of legitimacy bestowed by democracy. On one level, the role of our political institutions and law-giving process must have an element of the community making decisions about what it thinks is permissible behaviour. But in a liberal system the scope of this moralising was tightly constrained through the fear that the will of the majority would assert itself in a manner that was tyrannical.

* * *

One of the most significant casualties of this extension of the state has been the distinct sphere of human association that existed between the family and the political: civil society. This amorphous collection of forms of association, ranging from charities to sports clubs to churches, has found itself increasingly subject to the regulation and legal intentions of the state. Worryingly the tendency to view democracy as an all legitimating ideal has seen increasing interference by the state in those aspects of the civil associations that they determine to be undemocratic. Associations that practice restricted membership are denied support by the state or worse, positively restricted in their behaviour. Any form of exclusivity is seen as fundamentally undemocratic. In the name of equality and democracy the law has been brought to bear to punish the expression of belief or to regulate the practices of civil associations.

At the same time as seeking to bend civil associations to its own vision of democracy the state has also increasingly taken to subverting these associations in the pursuit of its policy goals. By co-opting and funding charities the state pursues its goals while removing the independence of the association. Once this distinct area of human association becomes subject to state regulation or co-option then little else lies between the individual and the state but the notion of rights. We lose an important check or barrier between the state and its citizens. The monomania that sees government as the only form of collective activity or association is closely related to the desire to see the state act wherever a perceived ill is identified. This failure to see any form of social life beyond the state or the private business endeavour has deeply damaged the life of communities across the West.

An interesting parallel can be found in the erosion of the separation of church and state in social democratic societies. The view that religious principles are not a proper matter for enforcement by the coercive power of the state placed a clear limit on the will of a majority religion which would prefer to see their practices adopted across the polity. Religious groups were left free to proselytize and to persuade, but came to accept that they could not enforce their teaching through law applied by coercion. It is clear that this outlook has changed when it comes to many moral issues. It is no longer the case that politicians are willing to accept limitations on their use of the coercive apparatus of the state to impose their moral codes.

Increasingly the results of this are all too clear to see. High levels of petty regulation and surveillance have been an alarming feature of the last two decades of political evolution. The police have become increasingly engaged with the implementation of a series of regulations designed to change the behaviour of individuals. Not the least of these has been the development of laws restricting free speech under the aegis of hate crimes, health related projects such as the smoking ban, or moral strictures concerned with the treatment of animals. Each of these regulations has been accompanied by the provision of an enforcement regime. Officials are given the power to police the regulation though surveillance or the issuance of fines. More troublingly they often involve granting the policing authority the right to enter property or examine private correspondence or bank details.

This ties in with an increasing tendency to infringe property rights. Not only is the use of property more tightly regulated than ever before, but what we can do in the comfort of our own home has increasingly come to be considered fair game for political interference. This is troubling from a liberal perspective as the security of property rights is the historical engine that has driven the economic and technological growth that has allowed the West to develop the standard of living that it enjoys today. Security of property combined with the protection of an extensive private sphere of individual activity encouraged the innovation and productivity characteristic of the West from the eighteenth century onwards. When the centrality of secure property rights to the defence of liberty and to the promotion of economic welfare is unappreciated, there is a real danger that it will be sacrificed in the name of democratically justified law and policy.

* * *

One of the conceptual incoherencies that plagues theories of modern democracy is that its lack of respect for property rights and individual autonomy strikes at one of the necessary conditions for a successful deliberative process. A society that does not value and protect individual property ownership cannot long remain a meaningful democracy. A free and independent citizenry is essential for the efficient operation of the kind of democracy proposed by Rousseau and his philosophical descendants. When the citizens find their views and lives subject to the interference of an executive enforcing the will of a democratic majority we lose the idea of a responsible citizen bringing his considered opinions to the political realm. Instead we are left with an increasingly dependent and supine populace willingly subjecting themselves to the dictates of the executive.

Elections are good things because they have provided us with a way of holding our governors to account while at the same time providing a trigger for the peaceful change of government. But the legitimacy granted by a democratic mandate has had the fatal effect of extending the legitimate scope of state activity in illiberal directions. This extension of political activity can know no bounds if democracy is the sole foundation of governmental legitimacy. The state will expand and expand its activities in the name of the people. And with these extensions comes the ever greater threat that the political institutions of our society will over-extend themselves. They will try to do too much in the name of the good of the people. As this happens there is an increasing risk that the institutional over-reach will lead to failures of delivery. And that failure of delivery will lead to an electorate disappointed by broken promises. This will undermine confidence in the state, leading to increased dissatisfaction with our political institutions.

The incentives created by a democratic polity have led to the growth of state activity and this in turn is paving the way for a crisis of legitimacy as the state fails to deliver on its extravagant promises while at the same time increasing the level of petty regulation and interference. The end result of increasing levels of policy-driven law and regulation has been the criminalisation of more and more activities. The more laws we have the greater the chance of breaking them and the larger the number of criminals we produce. Moreover, we also run the risk of de-legitimising law itself. Individuals harassed by state officials in their everyday activity, or overcome by red-tape, or fenced in by petty regulation will come over time to have little but contempt for the law and for those whose job it is to enforce it. The result of this is that we are approaching a crisis of legitimacy. And this crisis is not being precipitated by a lack of democracy, but rather it is a direct result of democracy itself. A democracy that forgets that politics is a limited activity — one that forgets the lessons of liberalism — will be well on the way to bringing about its own downfall.

Democracy has blinded us to the reality that politics is about coercion. Every state regulation and policy involves an exercise of coercion by the state towards its citizens. In exercising its power, democracy not only undermines the liberal foundations of a society, but renders many of its own citizens at best resentful and at worst supine — a classic symptom of the very tyranny that democracy is supposed to prevent.

Chapter Four

Democracy and the Big State

In the twentieth century modern democracy came of age. As a form of government it is now the bedrock of political life in the countries of the West where it originated, is the default system in much of South America, Asia and Africa, and is also aspired to almost everywhere else. Even those tyrannies which in practice resist democracy subscribe to its form. Most dictators claim the legitimacy of the ballot box even as they rig it. The few remaining countries that deny the sovereignty of the voter — certain traditional kingdoms such as Saudi Arabia or Bhutan, or Communist republics such as China — see the need to construct the artifice of popular consultation. There is enormous pressure everywhere for regimes to seek legitimacy in majority support from the population. There is global acceptance of this particular Western idea, even if other of its nostrums and institutions are questioned or rejected.

Yet if it is now taken for granted that democracy is the legitimate form of government, its essential features are surprisingly ill-understood. As we have discussed, democracy is usually thought of, in the West at least, as a guarantor of popular liberty. It is common for politicians and other commentators in the West to talk of 'Democracy and Liberty' in one phrase, as if the two go hand in hand. Indeed, in the various Western interventions in the Middle East and elsewhere around the turn of the Century, a primary objective has been to establish democracy as a means of entrenching essential freedoms on the Western model.

But as we established in the previous chapters, democracy is based not on the rights of the individual but the sovereignty of the majority. It is a method of appointing rulers, but in itself places few restrictions on how they treat the ruled. Curiously this mismatch between democracy and liberty is understood in practice much better outside the West, where there are plenty of examples of regimes that are democratic without being remotely liberal. Iran, for example, has a sophisticated constitution that has layers of popular representation while scorning the institutions of liberty. India was for a long time hailed as the largest democracy while its economy laboured under the most restrictive bureaucratic practices.

Far from entrenching liberty, the advent and establishment of democracy has relegitimised the power of the state, allowing it to flourish once more. The actions of government—until recently regarded with suspicion, and constrained by law and the instinctive hostility of voters—have acquired new validity. This chapter looks at the practical implications of the re-emergence of Big Government. For not since the heyday of the doctrine of the Divine Right of Kings has the executive governed with such confidence. After a relapse of three centuries the state has at last found a new sponsor. Not God this time, but the People. It is as if those paladins of classical liberalism imagined the universal franchise as a final nail in the coffin of tyranny, only to see it splinter the box and release the demon once more.

For not only has democracy brought new legitimacy to the state, it has introduced perverse dynamics in favour of state activism. The elected executive not only has the justification for intervention, but the incentive for Big Government too. We have already discussed the increasing erosion of individual rights under democracy. We now turn to how the scope and cost of government activity has exploded at the same time. The clearest way of measuring state power in a modern society is the level of taxation, though the increase in regulation is once more supplanting tax as the coercive tool of choice for government. The twentieth century saw a steep rise in levels of government spending in all of the major democracies. This process began with the establishment of universal suffrage in the countries of Western Europe and North America in the decades around 1900. It is now under way in the newer democracies of Eastern Europe, so recently liberated from the tyranny of Communism. The new legitimacy democracy bestows on government explains why the rise in taxation meets such little popular resistance on grounds of principle. Meanwhile the voters and government collude in the expansion of the state. Politicians, voters and civil servants respond to clear incentives inherent in a democratic political system, as the public choice economists observed (see Chapter Two).

The political motive is to 'buy' the votes of the electorate by redistributing wealth towards groups of voters large and diverse enough to provide a majority for re-election. As the economist Milton Friedman described,

> Throughout recorded history whenever leaders have been chosen by some method of voting, the aspirants for leadership have bought votes. Traditionally they have bought votes either with their own money or with a patron's money. To some extent they still do so. But something new has been added. Since the 1930s, the technique of buying votes with the voter's own money has been expanded to an extent undreamed of by earlier politicians (1985, p. 49).

So voters have a powerful incentive to choose parties or politicians who will benefit them most financially, whether through direct transfers or employment as civil servants. Thus electoral pressures lead to the formation of political coalitions able to turn the apparatus of government, especially the taxing, service providing and benefit distributing elements of the state's activities, to their advantage.

It is fair to say that the same dynamic places a natural limit on the power of the state to tax and spend. As soon as it becomes easier to build a coalition that benefits from *lower* taxation, the process is reversed as politicians seek electoral advantage by offering to cut taxes, and find it easier to win votes by doing so. This is why the overall level of taxation as a proportion of economic output in democracies fluctuates in the 35% to 50% range. As long as income inequality exists, and a majority remain net recipients of tax-and-spend, taxes tend to rise. But if taxes go much above 50%, an ever greater number become net losers from the tax / benefit system. Incentives in the electoral cycle go into reverse until levels of tax fall again.

In almost all Western countries, government expenditure as a proportion of the economy has risen dramatically in the democratic age. At the end of the nineteenth century, tax levels stood at between five and fifteen percent of gross domestic product in the nations of Western Europe, North America and Australasia. By the end of the twentieth rates typically stood at forty percent or more. The two world wars exacerbated the trend, which was briefly reversed in their aftermath before the cycle reasserted itself. It only levels out as the fifty percent barrier is approached. Such a limit might provide comfort to some. But to the liberals of eighteenth and nineteenth century Britain and America, the idea of taxes being permanently fixed in this range would have provoked horror.

Moreover, this limit on the state's ability to tax leads to a further dynamic in the mechanisms of democracy. The incentive remains to reward constituents with economic benefits while escaping the blame for the cost of doing so. This explains the shift in redistribution from traditional tax-and-spend to regulation, especially of non-voting entities such as companies. Simply ordering companies to increase wages using mechanisms such as a minimum wage or paternity leave hides the cost of a benefit while distributing it to plenty of voters. In the United States, the phrase 'pork barrel' politics was coined to describe how senators and congressmen acted to 'bring home the bacon' for their constituents. Typically they would attempt to win federal funds for voter-friendly projects close to home, or attach their name to a redistributive piece of legislation. Because federal spending is financed by the US as a whole, voters in a particular state feel a large benefit at the expense of a small cost. They tend to credit their own representative

with securing the benefit, while blaming the federal government for the rise in taxation that is the cumulative result of
all politicians acting in the same manner. Again, the incentive is at its most powerful when there is the opportunity to
bestow a benefit without a commensurate tax increase. And
here an additional trick for hiding taxes comes into
play — granting a benefit at one tier of government while
foisting the tax increase onto another. This ploy is used
wherever the fiscal boundary between different levels of
government is indistinct. In Britain it is most commonly
seen in a slightly different form to the US. Central government keeps taxes down by passing the responsibility for
funding benefits it has already bestowed to local authori-
ties, who must raise local taxes to pay for the privilege. The
relentless rise in Council Tax since its introduction in 1993 is
mainly due to this process.

So democratic government results in a remorseless cycle
of taxation and regulation. This is not to say that all politicians and all voters want to see interventionist redistribution on such a scale, nor that all those in political life act
purely with the cynical intention of buying power or 'rent
seeking'. But the dynamic of democracy leads inevitably to
a high tax, high intervention state, whatever the country
and whatever the political party in power at any one time.
An apologist for democracy, whether consciously echoing
the tradition of Rousseau or not, would argue that this outcome reflects the aggregated will of the majority of people,
and so is a just result, both in terms of legitimacy and in
moral terms. After all, is not poverty effectively redressed in
the modern West by democratic socialism? We have
already seen how democracy, in its assault on the sovereignty of the individual, undermines the civil liberties that
our forefathers fought so long to obtain. As such its legitimacy is no stronger in philosophical terms than that of the
old monarchies or modern tyrannies. Democracy merely
gives a veneer of legitimacy to the use of coercion. Yet any
system of redistribution that relies on force has no moral
validity. You gain no moral credit by robbing Peter to pay
Paul.

What is worse, Paul is not helped much either. As we have seen, the story of democratic government in the twentieth century is largely the story massive redistribution of wealth towards the poorer half of society. Yet this has failed to achieve its goals despite the most propitious of circumstances. Twentieth century governments in the West benefited from the enormous increase in material prosperity generated by the development of liberal market capitalism. When they were not fighting wars, they spent most of their time constructing mechanisms to spread this largesse among the populace in order to satisfy the electorate and eliminate poverty once and for all.

Political debate over the last hundred years has usually focussed on how redistribution can be justified in theory and implemented in practice. The traditional role of government — implementing foreign policy, defence and justice — while remaining important, has been eclipsed in terms of the time and resources government devotes to it. The resulting system in Britain called the Welfare State, has utterly failed to eliminate poverty, and has resulted instead in urban blight, high taxes, shoddy public services, and alarming levels of crime.

The essential truth is that poverty in Western societies is nothing to do with material wealth, or the absence thereof. The great general increase in wealth *should* be more than enough to save all but a tiny minority from the historic human curses of hunger, poverty and associated ill health. Indeed, those that we call poor now are in material terms perfectly well off by any historic standard or by comparison to those in third world countries. However, their circumstances and behaviour in many respects mirror those of our impoverished forebears and neighbours. What we might call 'artificial poverty' is the product of democratic socialism.

Redistribution of wealth may be common to most democracies, but it is delivered differently from country to country. In each it grew in response to the same general democratic incentives, but haphazardly and in varying forms according to the subtly different institutional makeup and cycles of political pressure and decision making that occurred from place to place. Generally speaking, though, there are four methods of distributing welfare. Benefits can be delivered in cash or kind, and they can be targeted to certain groups or universally distributed.

As we saw in Chapter One, the great explosion of prosperity in the nineteenth and twentieth centuries was driven by competitive market capitalism, based on the bedrock liberal institutions of property rights and the rule of law. Competition, both for investors in capital markets, and for customers in product markets, forces providers of goods and services to search continually for improvements in quality, technology and cost. It is the prime driver of increased wealth and economic growth.

The great twentieth century comparator was the USSR and other communist states which deliberately and systematically eschewed markets and therefore meaningful competition. The effects were disastrous, and the resulting collapse of communism a triumphant vindication of liberal market capitalism as a superior way of distributing resources and encouraging growth. It seems amazing, therefore, that Western countries persevere with the same Soviet-style approach for huge sections of their economies. For one of the major components of the welfare state is for governments to take over important industries and deliver their services for 'free at the point of delivery' (or with heavy subsidies attached). In other words, benefits are paid in kind. The pattern of such state ownership varies from country to country, but typically goods and services such as healthcare, housing, education, utilities, transport and even certain foodstuffs are distributed in this way in supposedly advanced Western democracies, sometimes universally, and sometimes targeted to certain 'deserving' groups. In Britain, for example, the healthcare and school education systems are state owned monopolies providing their services largely free at the point of delivery, as is a big section of the housing industry. The British National Health Service is one of the biggest employers in the world. Together these two, with social housing, account for some fifteen per cent of GDP.

In these sectors, users have lost the right to choose which hospital they want to seek treatment in, or to which school to send their children. Given our experience of the twentieth century communism, it is no surprise that the result has been that all three services are characterised by poor quality, low productivity, lack of innovation, and rationing. These industries are exempt from competitive pressures. Being protected monopolies, the National Health Service and the schools are not exposed to consumer choice. Similarly, owned as they are by the government, they are largely immune from investor pressure to improve performance. No taxpayer can sell his 'ownership' of the NHS to invest elsewhere.

In other words the reason behind their sub-standard performance is that Britain's health and education services share many of the characteristic inefficiencies of the old Soviet economy. To illustrate the point, imagine if the same structure of state-owned monopoly provision of goods and services 'free at the point of delivery' was extended to other areas of the economy as it was in the USSR. The provision of food, for example, is an even more important necessity than health or education. You would have thought it were a prime candidate for state production and distribution if this were the best model to alleviate poverty. But if supermarkets were run in this way, they would be afflicted by supply problems and rationing. Shoddy goods would be provided in the wrong quantities as the bureaucracy sought to meet consumer demand. Queues would become commonplace, as would poor service in drab surroundings.

In the NHS, this nightmare is often a reality. The NHS consistently ranks poorly compared to other countries' health systems, both in overall attainment and life expectancy, as well as in specific areas such as waiting lists, and access to hi-tech equipment, surgery and physicians. Moreover, health services are not just about keeping people alive. Patients want comfort and good service while they are undergoing treatment. All too often the NHS does not provide this. Amazingly, mixed sex wards are commonplace in Britain. And so bad is the food in NHS hospitals, for example, that discomfort spills over into malnutrition and additional health problems. Meanwhile the NHS suffers from serious problems of productivity. The big increases in state spending in the first few years of the twenty-first century resulted in declining productivity. In other words much of the money was wasted. And as with state owned industries the world over, the NHS suffers from a severe disconnection between owners, managers and the workforce. The reason is that the workforce enjoys political leverage over its government owners who cannot escape (as ordinary shareholders can) by taking their investment elsewhere. Through union action the workforce can cause a political crisis by threatening to bring the whole industry to a standstill. Such workforces become resistant to change, and government attempts at reform develop into bitter, divisive and often inconclusive battles fought out in the media spotlight. These features combine to undermine staff morale, creating a workforce who feel unloved and subject to constant upheaval.

The NHS exhibits another classic trait that is common to services that are 'free at the point of delivery', again familiar from communist countries. The consumer of such services has no incentives towards husbandry or tailoring his behaviour to minimise use. Instead he is encouraged to be as wasteful as he likes. In the case of healthcare this has very serious consequences because the system imposes no financial penalty on pursuing an unhealthy lifestyle. Access to medical attention costs the same (nothing) for someone whose behaviour is likely to cost the system more because he smokes or drinks too much, as for someone who does neither. In Britain there is a growing problem where the health gains of improved science are being undermined by obesity, excessive drinking and low fitness levels. These are likely to impose enormously increased costs on the health service in the future, as well as piling on the misery of ill-health to many in later life.

The problem is that these soviet-style state owned monopolies lack the price signals to allocate resources efficiently, the incentives to improve service, and the cost consciousness to promote consumer husbandry. Monopoly public services are periodically subject to reform as part of a cycle of government regulation, failure and retrenchment. Britain under New Labour and the subsequent Conservative/Liberal coalition made serious attempts to reform some public services. As we discuss in the next chapter, at different times, in different sectors, and in different jurisdictions, the exact character of monopoly public sector service provision varies. But the underlying problem of state provision is an enduring feature of democratic government.

State provision of education suffers from similar problems. For example, Scottish education was one of the great products of the liberal age. Building on a tradition of mass literacy with its roots in the Reformation, and its network of five medieval universities, the Scots developed an educational ethic and institutional base way in advance of England or the rest of Europe in the eighteenth century. Financed by fees or philanthropy, independent in outlook and rigorous in academic application, Scotland's schools and universities made a mighty contribution to the intellectual, military and economic prowess of the British Empire, producing generations of talented innovators in every field.

The rise in wealth and its resultant diversion of resources into schooling should now be putting Scottish schools at the top of the tree once again. But, nationalised in the mid twentieth century, Scottish school education now has all the hallmarks of state monopoly provision and the problems associated with it — lack of choice, poor productivity and low quality. By dint of a long tradition of pork barrel politics in which Scottish politicians have succeeded in winning ever greater funding relative to the other parts of the UK, public expenditure in Scotland is among the highest in the world as a proportion of GDP. In the first decade after devolution (when in 1999 power over education, healthcare and other domestic matters was granted to a new Scottish parliament) schools enjoyed a funding increase of more than

50% in real terms. The huge rise in funding since devolution resulted in little improvement in exam results, while international surveys showed the performance of Scots pupils declining against their counterparts elsewhere in the developed world. In other words, most of the extra money pumped in was wasted. In particular, there is a great discrepancy of quality between the top and the bottom in Scottish state schooling. As a result, many Scots are prepared to pay double (in taxes for the state system, then in fees) to escape state school and send their children to costly independents. Many more parents would do the same if they could afford to.

Meanwhile, in the state system, many parents operate in a 'shadow market' where they pay considerable sums to move house to more expensive areas where there are better schools. In other words good schools, both private and state, command a very high financial premium. There is no overall capacity problem (the numbers of schoolchildren are declining), so the only explanation for this is that the remainder of schools are not good enough. Rates of truancy, bad behaviour in schools, staff morale and low levels of literacy all highlight what the wealthy are trying to buy their way out of.

Governments face yet further problems when providing monopoly public services 'in kind'. They have no real way of telling how much to spend on them. Arguably, for example, in a rich country the proportion spent on health should be low. Health is a basic service, and once a country becomes rich it can afford to spend more on leisure goods and services. But what of the opposite view? Perhaps healthcare, like food, really is a luxury industry, where the basics needed to keep people alive are relatively cheap. For example in wealthy countries people want more than that — meals provided by smart restaurants or digital entertainment in single bed wards.

But we have no way of knowing whether this is justified or not. Should it be more on health and less on education? Or should taxes rise so more is spent on both, leaving people to spend less on housing, food, clothing and leisure? The politicians' only guide in this is the crude verdict of the electorate at general elections. Even opinion polls do not offer much of a clue, because they just reflect the public's desire to spend more on everything but less overall. In fact it is only the public, in the form of millions of individuals, that is capable of taking these decisions correctly. They are the experts at judging value for money, and the risks and rewards of alternative decisions. There is no way that civil servants and politicians, however numerous or clever they are, can make these myriad choices on behalf of millions of citizens.

We have looked at the problems encountered by societies that redistribute wealth through the provision of services in kind. There is a further set of problems that arise when welfare is 'targeted' at groups thought to be particularly needy. The fundamental problem with targeting welfare is that it introduces incentives for people to fall within the targeted group — in other words by deliberately 'failing' in order to qualify for state assistance. These false incentives do not affect the whole of society. The benefits on offer are obviously not sufficient to affect those whose income or circumstances are comfortable without receiving them. In the affluent West this is the majority. Nor is their worst effect on the truly destitute who would be incapable of surviving without some kind of help, perhaps through physical incapacity or ill luck in poor economic circumstances. For this small group state benefits have replaced charitable ones, and perform an essential function, if inefficiently. Instead, the false incentives offered by targeted benefits affect those for whom the decision on whether to seek benefits is marginal. This is a minority in society, but the great majority of those in receipt of such benefits. The system has seriously deleterious affects on this group, and indirectly on society as a whole.

Take a classic example which is very common throughout the advanced democracies. Benefits are typically available to those who cannot find work. Anyone in receipt of such benefits who then enters employment loses them. Therefore there is obviously a powerful disincentive to

enter work. The job in question would have to be suffi-
ciently well paid or interesting to compensate, not just for
the lost benefit but also for the time it took up and the leisure
opportunities it removed.

The effects of this are pernicious. For one, it damages the
economy. Many people avoid work, denying their labour to
the economy and increasing the overall tax burden to pay
for their benefits. It also forces wages upwards artificially as
employers must pay more to attract workers off welfare.
Indeed, Western governments have taken to setting a 'minimum wage' partly to encourage people off benefits in a classic case of 'double intervention'. This upward pressure on
wages, unjustified by any productivity increase, undermines the competitiveness of the economy as a whole.

Perhaps worse is the social impact of such benefits. Most
people would agree that jobless dependency on handouts is
undesirable. Many rightly feel guilty at relying on
unearned cash provided by someone else. Handouts undermine this ethic and encourage people to justify living off
benefits to themselves. A culture of entitlement rather than
duty creeps in, in a trend symptomatic of democratic socialism. This trend is enhanced by the fact that benefits are
received from the state, which passes no moral judgment on
the recipient, and has little incentive to question the legitimacy of the recipient's claim. By contrast, if the handout
comes from an independent source, whether the family,
friends, or institutions of civil society such as insurance
companies, co-ops or mutuals, the donor has a constant
incentive to encourage the recipient to pay his own
way — not just because of their concern from the well-being
of the recipient but in their own financial interests too. State
benefits tend not just to change the recipients' view of work
and dependency, but also undermine the function and purpose of healthier social networks and liberal institutions
such as the family, friendships and the old self-help organisations of civil society that are described in Chapter One.

If targeted benefits damage society, and benefits in kind
are inefficient, what of that unhappy group of benefits that
are both targeted and in kind? The most obvious example of

this is social housing, properties owned by local municipalities and rented to targeted groups on the basis of need. Provided by the state, social housing suffers from the all the problems of resource misallocation and waste that typify state provision. Government housing is notoriously poorly built and maintained. Neither landlord nor tenant has proper incentives to good design or maintenance. The state as owner / landlord has no shareholders to insist on efficient rent collection, no imperative to control costs and ensure viable revenue streams. It suffers little competition to spur its efforts, because its offering is subsidised by the taxpayer. In short it has a captive customer base for whom poor quality and design is outweighed by the financial advantages of the benefit on offer. This is not to speak of the enormous environmental damage caused by council housing. Cities across the democratic West are blighted by ghettos of social housing.

Meanwhile targeting ensures that those most vulnerable to benefit dependency, and the social problems that it brings, tend to cluster in council housing, making them ghettos of crime and social breakdown. Anyone familiar with *les banlieus* of urban France or the housing estates and programmes of inner city Britain and America will know that their social effect is similarly insidious. Where help with accommodation comes from family or friends, there are usually strings attached which force recipients to consider their options carefully. Young people reliant on their parents need to moderate their behaviour accordingly, whether it be with maintaining the property, going out at night or even starting a family. With no-strings help on offer from the state, there is not just less incentive to find work, but fewer incentives to conform to the mutual interests of family arrangements.

One of the most discussed effects of targeted benefits is the removal of incentives that encourage unitary family life. Before the arrival of state benefits, there were huge financial incentives for parents of young children to stay together. Co-operation between two adults was needed to cope with the dual demands of bringing income to the household and bringing up the children. Successful marriage or partnership is not built just on financial considerations, of course. But the social ethic that encourages marriage has its roots in its material benefits. No extended family or community wants to have to cope with a single mother and her offspring, so marriage has from the beginnings of humanity been encouraged as the preferred family state. The crucial by-product of marriage is that children are more likely to be better brought up because of the dual and contrasting influences of mother and father. There are clear links between the benefits system, the break down of family life, and social ills such as poor educational attainments, crime and drug abuse. Similar problems of false incentives exist with all targeted benefits, to the detriment of society's natural remedies to welfare problems and therefore its own cohesion.

Providing welfare in kind leads to enormous problems of quality and efficiency. Meanwhile targeting welfare to specific groups creates false incentives that encourage dependency. Together, these are not just economically expensive, but highly damaging to the natural structures of society and human behaviour that promote cohesion and encourage people to lead fulfilling lives.

The result is that Western societies are saddled with an enduring problem of social breakdown that has many of the hallmarks of real poverty. This raises the question: is it possible to design a welfare state that avoids the problems of state monopoly ownership and targeting? The obvious antidote is to distribute welfare in cash universally, to all citizens. In theory this would avoid the disincentives and poverty traps of targeting, while allowing the efficiencies of market economics to improve public services. Citizens would use their cash benefits to buy health, education, housing and the rest from competing private sector providers. In fact there are numerous examples of welfare provision in democracies that approximate to this. An obvious example in Britain is the provision of child benefit, which all but the wealthiest parents receive and can use freely to buy essentials for their children from ordinary private suppliers. The next chapter discusses this concept in more detail because it is an important part of the balance that is struck within democracy between liberalism and socialism. But even such an approach to welfare does not avoid the increasing cycle of intervention by government in the economy and society. In shouldering responsibility for redistribution and welfare, democratic government acquires an interest in the way it is delivered and also in economic and social outcomes.

As social and economic failures become apparent, whether as a direct result of intervention or not, governments come under increasing pressure to intervene; 'something must be done'. It is becoming increasingly apparent that this problem has sinister implications for our society that go beyond economic meddling. The government's response to 'irresponsible' lifestyles that lead to unsatisfactory outcomes is to regulate them. This poses serious dangers to the moral, as well as material well-being of individual citizens.

We have already touched upon this problem in Chapter Three but it is worth exploring its practical consequences in greater detail here. Individuals have become increasingly dependent on the state as both a service provider and a regulator of preferred forms of behaviour in society at large. Society's material and moral self-reliance has been endangered as a result. Bans on smoking in public places are an obvious recent example of this, but Western governments regularly threaten, variously, to restrict the sale of alcohol, ban certain foods, or even restrict medical treatment to those lacking in lifestyle virtue.

A few years ago, such interventions would have been dismissed as an unwarranted interference in the private choices of adults. The disastrous example of alcohol prohibition in the US was still remembered. But the justification is now that such behaviour imposes a wider social cost. A common argument from people who support the smoking ban is that they do not want to pay for the cost of treating smokers through higher taxes. The system of financing the NHS, therefore, as well as the poor quality of its outcomes, provokes unwarranted government intervention in people's private lives in a vicious circle of interference. The smoking ban and the arguments around it are darkly reminiscent of public policy in the nastier dictatorships of the last century.

Bans and restrictions do not just attack the margins of personal liberty in our society, they also undermine personal responsibility. Citizens who need not choose between certain courses of action eventually lose the capability to make sensible economic and social decisions for themselves. This was one of the main problems faced by the Soviet Union when it tried to switch to a capitalist model in the 1990's. Many of its citizens found it very difficult to adjust to a life where they had to make important choices about work and lifestyle. Indeed many voters in ex-communist countries still hanker after the childhood-like security of state decision making despite the obvious long term damage it inflicts.

The moral and material problems of welfare dependency clearly affect most severely that segment of the population that is most dependent on benefits and suffers most from the inefficiencies of state provision. Usually this is the same group of people. Those dependent on benefits are least able to work the system to avoid the worst in state education and healthcare. Wealthy people move house to live near the better state schools. Their children secure a better education, and rich, well educated people are better at tackling the bureaucracy to secure faster and better medical attention.

It is difficult to put a figure on the proportion of the population that exists in 'artificial poverty'. The political commentator Will Hutton spoke of a '30%/30%/40%' society, implying that nearly a third of the population is artificially poor. This might seem extreme. But a combination of those who suffer from illiteracy, economic inactivity, chronic ill-health or exposure to low level disorder makes up a sizeable proportion of the population. Moreover, there is not a complete overlap between these different groups, and many people are directly affected by these conditions even if they do not appear in the statistics. They may be related to those who are, or live in areas, blighted by crime. In all, therefore, a 25%-30% figure for 'artificial poverty' rates seems reasonable.

However, failures in welfare mar the whole nation, and indirectly affect most citizens. Economically, a malfunctioning welfare state is very expensive. Productivity in state controlled industries is low, implying enormous financial waste. Targeted welfare increases worklessness and distorts the labour market. The effect of crime and disorder in society is even more worrying. There can be no doubt that the rise in crime in the twentieth century is intimately connected with the breakdown of social networks that has been caused, or at least worsened, by the welfare state. As the source of welfare has shifted from personal thrift and voluntary institutions such as family, friends or charity to the state, the authority and natural discipline of those institutions has been undermined.

This has had a dramatic impact on crime, especially low level crime, that the state has difficulty in controlling. Anti-social activity such as vandalism, petty theft and burglary, gang membership and public disturbances are best policed by the moral and financial controls that families and small communities hold over their members. When this control is undermined by state welfare, the state must step in as an alternative authority, and it has great difficulty in doing so.

What we are witnessing is a cycle of intervention whose genesis lies in the political dynamic inherent in democracy that leads to the redistribution of wealth via the welfare state. As the intrinsic contradictions that this entails lead to worse outcomes, the state is encouraged into ever more intervention, whether through direct ownership of service providers, or greater regulation of institutions and lifestyles.

Chapter Five

The Return of Market Liberalism

In September 2002, the British Labour Prime Minster Tony Blair made a remarkable confession in a pamphlet written for the Fabian Society:

> Our public services, despite the heroic efforts of dedicated public servants and some outstanding successes, are not all of the quality a nation like Britain needs (2002, p. 1).

He went on to identify the problem and suggest market competition as a solution:

> Choice is crucial both to individual empowerment and — by enabling the consumer to move to an alternative provider where dissatisfied — to quality of service (*Ibid.*, p. 20).

This extraordinary epiphany — coming from the leader of a political movement that was the prime driver of democratic socialism in Britain throughout the twentieth century — was the culmination of a big shift in the orientation of British politics. In essence the main socialist party seemed to be accepting that direct government intervention in the economy had failed, even in the provision of social welfare. For many, the conversion of 'New Labour' (as Blair had renamed his party) to market orthodoxy marked the final triumph in the resurgence of liberalism in Britain, at least in economic terms.

Yet not all welcomed this apparent new consensus. And in fact on closer inspection this liberal counter-revolution is proving to be ephemeral. This chapter explains how the liberal reforms that took place most noticeably in Britain and America after the end of the 1970's are part of the democratic political cycle.

Just as the level of taxation rises and falls within a band just under the 50% mark, so the level of intervention in the economy will fluctuate in response to voter reaction to economic and social developments. But the motor of democracy ensures that, over the longer term, government domination of key social and economic institutions remains. Typically, analysis of political trends in Britain and the US takes place in isolation (or in Britain externally with reference only to the US), so commentators often miss developments elsewhere in the democratic world that should help to reveal that the return of market liberalism is part of a repetitive cycle rather than a linear progression.

Blair's epiphany marked the formal conversion of Labour to market reform of the welfare state, yet he and his party were simply following a train of intellectual thought and political logic that had been set in motion decades before.

The crucial political events in both Britain and the US were the conversion of the main conservative parties to liberal market economics. This took place under a dual influence. Firstly, the performance of the 'commercial' economy (away from the welfare state) in both countries declined in relative terms in the post war period, as specific problems such as inflation, labour relations, unemployment and poor industrial management became increasingly prevalent. Secondly, a new intellectual movement developed that, while its foremost philosophers were academics, and some of its adherents politicians, found a neutral outlet in new 'think tanks'. In Britain, the Institute of Economic Affairs (founded 1955) and the Centre for Policy Studies (1974) and others acted as platforms for independent thinking that was propagated through the media and specialist publishing.

This combination allowed conservative politicians to explore liberal thinking on economics outside the context of formal politics (which might have stymied it) and allowed other 'opinion formers' such as journalists to buy into the new thinking without declaring a political allegiance.

In Britain the process was assisted by the final conversion of the electorally desperate Liberal party in the 1960s and 1970s to the socialist orthodoxy of the time, which made it politically easier for the Conservatives to occupy the vacant ground. The transformation of conservative politics in Britain and America was converted into a coherent government programme with the elections of Margaret Thatcher in 1979 and Ronald Reagan in 1980. In Britain the resurgence of liberal thought and practice took place in two distinct phases. The initial focus of the British Conservatives was to encourage market competition in non-welfare industries. A programme of labour market reforms, financial deregulation, privatisation and the lowering of marginal tax rates improved productivity in commercial sectors that had been heavily regulated or even owned by the government. Perhaps the most radical reform was of the utility sector, where gas and electricity companies were first privatised, and then broken up in an innovative new market structure that allowed competition at the production and retail levels. This went beyond anything achieved even in Victorian times.

These reforms were reluctantly accepted by Labour and the Liberals (who in 1981 merged with a breakaway faction of Labour to become the Liberal Democrats) in the late 1980s and 1990s. Yet the second phase of reform, applying liberal market theory to the welfare state, took place on a different timetable. For many years now, Conservative politicians have understood how, in principle, competitive markets could be extended into welfare without threatening poorer citizens' access to public services. They saw that government could redistribute money to citizens in the form of vouchers that could be cashed with competing providers of health, education, housing, pension plans and the rest. These ideas had been proposed in Britain and America since at least the early 1960s. They achieved global prominence with Milton Friedman's *Free to Choose* television series in 1980. This approach promised to extend the huge productive benefits of market capitalism to public services, without undermining the redistributive function of the Welfare

State. But throughout the long governments of Thatcher and Major (1979–97), and despite successful market reforms elsewhere in the economy, they largely failed to implement this agenda in the face of bitter political opposition.

The critical breakthrough came with the election of Tony Blair. It is not that his administration was particularly effective at implementing market reforms of welfare. Indeed it spent its first term reversing the previous government's belated and tentative attempts at creating internal markets in health and education. It was not until half way through New Labour's time in office that it made limited progress introducing university tuition fees, allowing greater school independence and instituting limited choice in the health sector. More importantly, the conversion of New Labour swung the political balance in favour of reform, with the Liberal Democrats falling in behind. In essence this established a cross-party consensus in favour of reform, whereas previously market ideas had been associated with one party, the Conservatives, and thus opposed by everyone else. This opened up the possibility at least for future governments of whatever hue to attempt reforms in welfare, as the Conservative-Liberal Democrat coalition elected in 2010 demonstrated.

In his Fabian pamphlet Tony Blair even used the examples of utility liberalisation — so bitterly opposed by his own party a decade earlier — as a model to describe the benefits of applying liberal market theory to welfare provision:

> In the private sector, people increasingly have an incredible amount of choice over who provides their services — from gas supplies and broadband to insurance and air travel. Many of these markets, and the choice of suppliers within them, did not exist ten or twenty years ago. Public services have to respond to this world of much greater choice (Blair, 2002).

For the time being, then, British politics seemed to be heading along a liberal progression. It seemed to many commentators, on both the left and the right, that the post-war socialist experiment was a temporary aberration, with the inevitable reaction leading to the triumphant return of liberalism spurred by the necessity of market reform. Sadly, they were wrong. For the British experience is best seen as part of the ebb and flow of democratic politics, a constant cycle of political change that occurs within quite narrow bands set by the dynamic of democracy. Just as this manifests itself in levels of taxation, so it is apparent in the ever shifting programmes of activist governments.

In attempting to put their ideas on welfare into practice, British politicians looked abroad for practical models of how welfare could be delivered differently. For while the early Thatcherite reforms of the commercial economy were pioneering in the context of the late twentieth century, in welfare terms Britain has been a follower rather than a leader. It is this that demonstrates that the tug of war between market liberalism and socialism is a cycle rather than a progression.

Elsewhere in Europe, using markets and non-state institutions to deliver welfare is commonplace. One country admired by both Labour and Conservative politicians is Sweden, which used to have a welfare state very similar to Britain's, including state monopoly provision of health and education. Sweden undertook radical market reform of both around the turn of the century, and its impeccable Scandinavian social democrat credentials make it a safe and attractive precedent for British politicians to point to.

In healthcare, the democracies of continental Europe abound with a variety of different systems. Typically, healthcare is provided by a mixture of private, state, local authority or charitable institutions, backed up with government funding. In countries such as Germany, France or Belgium, citizens take out a health insurance policy which can be provided either by the government itself or by regulated private sector finance providers (often co-operatives). Sometimes premiums are administered through the payroll, sometimes paid by individuals (often wealthier ones who then reclaim it through their tax claims) and sometimes paid directly by government.

What all these systems have in common is that there exists a multiplicity of different providers, who compete either directly or by example, and often compete for private investment in the capital markets too. At the same time the government guarantees or finances access, so that a universal standard of healthcare is affordable by all.

Schools in continental Europe are often run on similar lines. In the Netherlands, for example, they enjoy considerable autonomy, with parents able to transfer their children with government money following their choices, a very similar system to that proposed by Milton Friedman all those years ago. The 'discovery' that continental European systems seem to have applied the market-based theories developed so agonisingly in Britain all along poses something of a conundrum to British politicians. For socialists, it is inconvenient that these social democratic continentals, so often held up as role models in the past, appear to adhere to the hated dogmas of Friedman and the Thatcherites.

But the real lesson is for liberals. The continental model of welfare is sometimes called the 'Bismarckian' model after the great German Chancellor who first attempted to accommodate the political dynamics of universal suffrage. It simply describes a different route whereby democracies embark upon the cycle of intervention. Continental Europeans do not see their welfare states as enshrining the eternal virtues of liberal market competition as the best way of distributing resources. Instead, the political pressures are constant in France, Germany and the rest to regulate, restrict and intervene.

Across Europe the ebb and flow of democratic socialism is constant. The pension system in Italy is an unaffordable, open ended benefit spree. The schools of France are becoming ever more centralised. The universities of Germany lost their independence long ago. The health systems of Europe, funded by social insurance schemes, may deliver better quality than that in Britain for the time being, but suffer from a spiral of increasing costs brought on in part by government regulation. Meanwhile transport and utility networks are usually state owned monopolies, and industry is routinely subject to intervention, protectionism and government ownership, in a way that shocks the market converts of Britain.

In America, while the initial liberal reaction to economic crisis via conservative politicians had many similarities with Britain, the experience of welfare reform has been very different. The US is often thought of in Europe as being a low tax, liberalised free-for-all with limited government intervention. But as we have seen it is in fact subject to the same inevitable cycle of intervention as other democracies. School education is, as in Britain, mostly run on socialist lines, on a model much less liberal than the European norm. Again like in Britain, the early twenty-first century saw the beginning of a trend to encourage independence and competition. But that is where the similarities end. Healthcare is by contrast at the other extreme, almost uniquely in democracies a largely private system in both ownership and finance. Unsurprisingly, here the trend is for the dynamic of democracy to reassert itself strongly. In 2010 the US government passed a bill to socialise healthcare, moving towards a compulsory insurance system similar to those in continental Europe. During the debate of this bill some US politicians even argued in favour of adopting the old British NHS model. Welfare in the US is different again, being fragmented along state lines, with liberal reforms taking place in some areas, and being undermined in others.

The picture throughout the mature Western democracies is one of flux — reform becomes politically expedient for a time as the contradictions of state control become particularly apparent in one sector or another. Then the incentives towards government activism reassert themselves as soon as the situation allows. But never do we see a complete, mechanistic return to liberalism. Instead the default position is for heavy government taxation and regulation of society.

The example of Britain shows how the motor of democracy works at different levels coincidentally. We have the bizarre situation where in some areas liberal reforms are promoted to tackle poorly performing sectors, while simultaneously recent reforms in others are undone as improved performance is taken for granted, and the lessons of failure forgotten. Towards the end of New Labour's time in office, the government was re-regulating utility and labour markets while at the same time liberalising education and health. The paradox shows that policy is not so much a product of party philosophy or principled leadership, as of natural reaction to the in-built incentives inherent in a democratic system of government.

We have already discussed the broad incentives towards big government. But there are a number of specific features of democratic socialism that make the return of market liberalism so ephemeral and prone to dilution. One of the features of socialism is that resources are diverted inefficiently, and this includes towards people. In other words, large numbers of those who work in socialised industries are effectively overpaid for the work they do, taking into account not just pay, but working conditions, pension arrangements, job security and management practices as well. This creates vested interests that are hostile to any reform that might undermine their material position. Such interests are mobilised by unions or politicians who are dependent on the public sector voters who make up a significant part of the electorate. This constituency continues to exist even once reform has successfully taken place. Life is cosier in the public sector, and employees of private sector companies that get into trouble often lobby for government takeover.

So despite the universal logic of reform, many have an individual logic in opposing it. Such individuals tend to use the language of socialist idealism which still has some resonance with the wider voting public. In particular they play on the public's dislike of inequality to claim that reform will leave many destitute (in the case of benefit reform) or with inadequate service (in the case of public sector reform). They also play on the perceived venality of profit making in the private sector, and will even point to public sector job losses caused by reform. Another favourite tactic is to point to incompetence, poor performance or corruption in the private sector, as if it were unique trait in organisations that are exposed to the pressures of competition and consumer choice.

In response the proponents of reform must change their language and methods as policies and positions become tainted by the endless battles with the forces of the status quo. Ways to describe the benefits and process of breaking state monopolies change bewilderingly. Words like 'privatisation' or 'vouchers' have become almost taboo, successfully associated by the nay-sayers with excess profits, 'fat cats' and the now-discredited Conservative governments of the 1980s and 90s. Their language has been 'decontaminated'. 'Competition' has been replaced by 'contestability', 'choice' by 'personalisation'. In their efforts to describe reform in a way that is palatable to voters, euphemism has become an art form.

If debate and language were the only barriers to reform, we might be further down the road. But other factors skew the political battleground against the reformers. One is inherent in the nature of monopoly. Customers rarely get the chance to sample an alternative, and so do not realise how bad their regular service is. This is clearly the case with health and education sectors, because few citizens experience medical care or education abroad, and there is little comparison with what the best has to offer. This explains why in Britain it was easier to reform the car maker British Leyland than the National Health Service. Many British people do not see the need for reform of the NHS because they have no tangible idea of what could be achieved by bringing in new ideas. It would appear that a large proportion of the population believes that the NHS really is the best health service in the world, and that hospital acquired infections, mixed wards, waiting lists and the like are normal.

At the same time, both health and education are rarely used. No voters experience school directly. Despite its huge cost, mercifully few voters are seriously ill or dependant on the health service for any length of time. This makes it both easier to oppose reform, and also to propose re-regulation once reform has taken place. Finally, the success of capital-

ism is to a certain extent self-defeating. The wealth generated by economic growth in the West has made it easier to
'carry' non-productive sectors of the economy. The great
increase in taxation of the first decade of this century in Britain was barely noticed by voters, even though the public
sector hardly improved as a result. It took the 2007 credit
crunch to expose the colossal overspend as voters were sud-
denly confronted with the requirement to reduce the deficit
with both tax increases and public spending cuts. The reason was that the dynamism of the competitive private sector, unleashed by earlier economic reform, was such that
disposable incomes increased despite the simultaneous
waste of tax and spend. It would seem that reform suffers
from the law of diminishing political returns.

The truth is that markets are seen as a tool by democratic
politicians to be adopted or rejected at need. The idea that
liberalism should be universally applicable, and that free
markets are an intrinsic part of a free society is misinter-
preted as a blind economic ideology. Democrats are so used
to wielding power that liberalism — the absence of state
power — is inconceivable to them. The ebb and flow of
reform and regulation is the norm, with market reforms
used as a pragmatic tool to achieve certain social or economic ends. This approach leads to serious institutional
problems in democratic societies. There is a trend of commercial structures being established that are designed to
achieve certain social objectives by exploiting market mechanisms. These 'were-markets' are neither exposed to free
competitive pressures, nor properly politically accountable.

The result is the creation of a web of false incentives that
can lead to institutions taking unsustainable risks with
potentially catastrophic consequences. Where businesses
take risks, but the state stays responsible, we see the creation a were-market. Neither fully state nor private, it
comes back to haunt society when least expected, and with
disastrous effects. The financial crisis of 2007 was a classic
case in point. It revealed a core imbalance in the Western
economy caused by the meshing of capitalism and democracy. The roots of the credit crunch went back as far as the

1930's, when in the wake of the depression the US government effectively underwrote the mortgage market through the creation of the federal mortgage agency Fannie Mae. Subsequent governments in the US, Britain and elsewhere have regulated the mortgage and banking markets to limit market entry and competition while encouraging lending through direct subsidies, artificially low interest rates or guarantees.

The political goals of this were-market are clear — to provide affordable housing, one of the most potent electoral weapons in the arsenal of the democratic politicians. The bankers (like politicians and every other rational agent subject to incentives) responded by lending more money than was prudent, knowing that in a democracy no government could let them go bust. They were 'too big to fail'. Such was the extent of the bubble that the finance was provided not by depositors, but by wholesale lenders, governments and banks from around the world, thus ensuring that the effects of the inevitable bursting of the bubble were felt globally.

Needless to say, the politicians have a strong motive to blame the banks, conveniently ignoring the fact that they themselves created the were-market by responding to similar incentives. In essence they were buying votes with cheap mortgages funded by the wholesale markets.

The reforming governments of the 80's, 90's and 2000s in Britain created a number of were-markets as the nostrums of market economics were inappropriately applied as tools to achieve various policy objectives. One example is the use of 'public private partnerships' where governments fund the infrastructure of state monopolies using the balance sheets of private banks. This is an attempt to deploy commercial disciplines in the running of public sector contracts. But as Adam Smith pointed out nearly three hundred years ago, in the absence of competition, the commercial incentive is the same as the public sector one — to maximise revenue by inflating costs.

The same unfortunate outcomes are seen time and again as government departments at all levels in Britain and other democracies hire private consultants to improve their internal practices. This attempt to buy in the disciplines of the market without understanding its essential component — competition — is like a man who buys a Lamborghini with the engine of a Morris Minor and expects it to drive fast.

The creation of were-markets by democracies not only creates systemic risks and poor management practices. It also undermines the reputation of liberal institutions and methodologies. The rip-off practices that are revealed when government and capitalism marry undermine popular trust in genuine competitive capitalism which, as Smith described, is the only effective, if unwitting, servant of the public interest. Thus the misapplication of commercial practices is another example of the dynamic of democracy at work. Liberal reforms lead to the corruption of liberalism, which in turn spurs the reaction against it. Ironically the creation of the were-market mirrors capitalist pastiches which are emerging elsewhere in the developing world, most notably in China.

Chapter Six

The Fall of the West

China is the outstanding example of a country that is copying aspects of Western society to its own advantage. By allowing private commercial property rights, encouraging private investment and creating markets for both investors and consumers, the Chinese economy has been able to deliver impressive levels of growth averaging nearly 10% over the last two decades. China is now the second largest economy in the world. The intention of the Chinese state is clearly to reverse two centuries of relative decline in the face of Western sophistication, and thus reassert China's place as a force to be reckoned with. Yet the Chinese model is deeply flawed, not just in terms of its autocratic style of government, but in the make up of its institutions and even the nature of its economic 'miracle'. It should be deeply worrying that the Chinese approach is seen by many, whether approvingly or not, to be the likely successful paradigm of the future.

For China behaves like one big were-market. The Chinese government has distorted almost every aspect of the economy to achieve its political end, which is rapid headline economic growth. It is using market capitalism as a policy tool. The result, as with all were-markets, is that unsustainable, unintended side-effects are being created that will damage society in the long run. By manipulating markets to deliver certain outcomes, the distribution of resources is uncontrollably skewed, just as the housing market was been in the USA and Britain in the run up to the 2007 credit crunch. Thus the Chinese government artificially devalues its state currency, the Renminbi, in order to boost demand for its exports as the prime driver of growth. This policy, consistently pursued over many years, has the effect of reducing incomes for Chinese workers (as well as undermining producers abroad). The fruits of economic growth are not enjoyed by Chinese people, but diverted into expanding manufacturing capacity. There is patchy insurance against old age, sickness, unemployment or the other hazards of life. Intellectual and social freedoms are suppressed.

At the same time, the natural by-products of rapid industrial growth have insufficient cost ascribed to them. Massive pollution, the destruction of architectural heritage, species loss and deforestation are all tolerated in the temple of headline economic growth. In other words, many of the aspects of human life that have real value are sacrificed for others, essentially because it is easier under conventional definitions to measure, say, exports or GDP growth than the risk of sickness or the existence of Yangtse river dolphins. Resources are not distributed according to worth in China. So the dramatic economic growth there is illusory, and the imbalances created will, as in all were-markets, eventually become manifest.

Yet in observing China, the West cannot be too self congratulatory, for it is looking into a mirror. The two societies are becoming ever more similar. The only real difference is on specific government objectives: The Chinese pursue reckless headline growth, while Western governments pursue a hotchpotch of social and economic ends in response to the electoral incentives described earlier in this book.

By contrast, in a free society, government has no objectives, bar the maintenance of the rule of law. This may require decisive interventions, particularly in the interests of upholding justice at home and defending the country from foreign threats. But in essence a liberal government is disinterested in outcomes. Instead, it is people who have objectives, and the purpose of government is to allow them to pursue these freely. This is not just a pragmatic notion, but a moral one, because government can only act using coercive force, wheras people act through free will.

Western countries have fallen far from this ideal. Everywhere, as in China, we see people and institutions being manipulated and corrupted to achieve certain government purposes. Thus they lose their vitality, their spontaneity, their capacity for innovation and therefore their productivity. There are many other areas where the rot has set in, sometimes with particularly serious consequences. Perhaps most worrying is the erosion of civil liberties in name of security — an area where the West's criticism of China is becoming increasingly hypocritical. We have already looked at how the dynamic of democratic socialism leads to the aggrandisement of the state. It results in a proliferation of laws and regulations, higher taxation, and greater intervention in the economy. But it is not just a question of the balance between free markets and state control of the economy that has shifted. As the legitimacy of the state has grown, so has its tendency to sweep aside the various constitutional restrictions that were imposed on it, as we suggested in Chapters Two and Three.

This tendency is now turned into reality. In Britain, legal rules designed to protect the individual, long fought for and cherished by our forebears, are being undermined. Trial by jury, that essential right that protects the citizen from arbitrary punishment by the state, has now been scrapped in certain cases. At the same time, the independence of the judiciary is continually questioned by democrats who see unelected judges as illegitimate barriers to the will of the people. In combination these two developments pose a serious risk to civil liberties and the rule of law, that are an uncomfortable reflection of practices in illiberal states such as China or Iran.

The assault on the legal foundations of liberty does not end there. In some cases now in Britain, the 'double jeopardy' rule has been waived, allowing the state to prosecute the same person twice for the same crime. The implication of this in the future is that the state will be able to dispense with verdicts it does not like.

Of course, for the present, each of these changes can be justified on grounds that exceptional cases require special measures. No-one yet seriously believes there is a plot by the politicians involved to take away individual rights. But the fact that a government can remove these rights on political grounds, because it does not approve of the outcome of the legal process, shows the dangers ahead. As does the seeming public indifference to these developments.

Such change provides a precedent which can be used by less scrupulous political leaders in the future. Good examples of such unintended consequences already exist. Measures taken to allow surveillance of potential terrorists are now routinely used by government agencies to check up on ordinary citizens to see if they have complied with minor local authority by-laws.

The pattern here is clear. As the state reasserts its legitimacy, it begins, perhaps unwittingly at first, to break the constitutional fetters that formerly bound it. So Western societies like Britain are slowly reverting to the pre-liberal conditions of arbitrary government power. And so they are becoming more like confessedly illiberal modern states such as China or Iran.

Just as with the corruption of market liberalism, the erosion of civil liberties risks the West losing its special advantages over other geopolitical models. As the arbitrary power of the state grows, so does its corruptions. And the ability of citizens to exploit economic and social opportunities to the benefit of all, and to live original, intellectually free, imaginative lives without the fear of prosecutions, diminishes.

For it is no coincidence that, as the power of the state grows in the democratic West, freedoms of thought, of belief and of expression are also being threatened. One of the critical battles that liberals fought and won against the tyrannies of old in Europe was for religious freedom. A powerful state holds a big advantage over its people if it can define the nostrums of belief. In the modern West it is increasingly frowned upon to express certain views, and in some cases actually illegal to act on them, even if no harm is done to others. We described in Chapter Three how certain types of behaviour are now restricted if they offend the moral sensibility of the governing class. This new development is extended to freedom of expression too. The idea is increasingly prevalent that opinions that cause offence to others must not be articulated. For the moment, this trend is largely confined to the margins of acceptable behaviour. So certain extreme interpretations of history are already outlawed, for example 'holocaust denial' in Germany and Austria. In Britain it is in some circumstances illegal to make utterances that can be construed to be 'racist' or 'homophobic', or to form associations or conduct business in a way that offends others.

The dangers of this should be obvious. The notion of what is offensive is open to interpretation, to an official view of what society regards as the norm. Future governments can extend this definition *ad infinitum*, and will be under pressure to do so from special interests looking for legal advantage. So the distinctions between 'religion' and 'race' are becoming increasingly blurred. A critic of a certain religion can be accused of 'racism', as if he were advocating that people be treated differently according to their physical characteristics. In essence, freedom of expression is relegated as a priority if it clashes with the government's social objectives, much as in a tyranny. And as with economic liberalism, elections alone are little defence against the erosion of freedoms because so many voters either have an interest in restricting the liberty of others, or else are not directly affected by it.

Even in the field of science, freedom of expression appears to be under threat. We are already seeing pressure from some quarters to place restrictions on criticism of the scientific consensus on climate change. This last development reflects a growing trend whereby academic institutions are losing their freedom in the democratic West. Again, one of the crucial elements of the liberal revolution was the development of universities and schools that were free from the clutches of organised religion or governmental sponsorship. This contributed to an intellectual tradition that encouraged original thought and the investigation of scientific and philosophical problems.

Research and education at the higher level is still a strength for Western societies. But as the growing state takes a greater interest in moulding society to suit its economic and social goals, it sees education as an essential tool in doing so. In most Western countries, the school system is either directly owned, or at least heavily regulated by the state. Curricula are set to universal norms that reflect the state's economic priorities and its philosophical outlook. Universities, where not controlled directly, are bullied or bribed to partake in the state's social engineering. And state patronage of university research leads to an enormous bias in favour of investigation that fits the state's view of society and its priorities.

In terms of social freedoms, it is true that the maturing of democracy coincided with the explosion of pop culture in the West, and the dissolution of many conservative social mores. Yet this does not demonstrate an increase in real freedoms, so much as a change in social fashion and conventions. This happens cyclically throughout history, as exemplified by the stuffy reaction of the Victorians to their libertine predecessors. The subsequent loosening of social bonds in our era was probably encouraged by the post war decades of peace and prosperity rather than any late bloom of liberty.

Besides, it is interesting to observe how, at the margins of pop culture, some behavioural symbols are succumbing to the new trend in civil restrictions. Smoking, swearing, high decibel levels, drinking and drug use (briefly espoused by the left as an antiestablishment activity before being crushed again on health grounds) and 'bad influences' are all under attack again. All this is leading to a blunting of free expression in the West, and a reversion to the norm where intellectual and social activity is controlled, and therefore its potential to discover new ways to pursue life is restricted.

We have already discussed how government becomes ever more interventionist in economic matters in response to the political incentives inherent in a democracy. Just like in China, market mechanisms are seen as a tool with which to achieve certain social, political and economic ends. One aspect of this is of particular concern. The establishment of secure property rights was a central element of the development of liberal societies in the West. The importance of property rights is usually seen these days in economic terms. Certainly, no market can function unless the parties involved can validate their possession of goods, services and property to be exchanged under secure contract that is proof against random sequestration by others. The work of development economists like Hernando de Soto has shown how the absence of secure property rights is the single biggest problem for third world countries. Citizens who do not own or securely lease their own home (let alone business premises, plant or intellectual property) find it difficult to raise finance, enter into employment contracts, trade, or even get utility connections. They also tend less to husbandry and development of their assets because they have no incentive to improve something that is not theirs.

It is often forgotten in the West that secure property rights are not just a piece of the economic jigsaw. As we have described, they are a crucial bulwark that protects individual freedom against a despotic state. They provide an arena, protected by the rule of law, in which the individual can build his life free from arbitrary interference by others. What became the essential tool of market capitalism began as an assertion of freedom.

But in the West, as in China, essential tools are increasingly thought of as there to be manipulated, used and discarded according to the political objectives of government. So while in China property rights have been established selectively in areas thought necessary to allow headline economic growth, in the West they are increasingly being eroded where they are seen as barriers to political goals. Again, the two societies are converging. In Britain, for example, private property is increasingly being opened up to access regardless of the permission of the property owner. 'Right to Roam' legislation allows the public to enter private land automatically. Even the home is subject to increasing powers of access by various government agencies, and the freedom to conduct legal activities at home that are frowned upon by the state (such as smoking) are under increased pressure. Again, an important pillar of liberty is being undermined wherever it gets in the way of the state's immediate political objectives.

This utilitarian approach to property rights is exemplified in both societies' approach to that modern shibboleth, the environment. The irony is that Western criticism of China is strident on environmental matters. Yet this is an argument not of principle, but of nuance — of one tyranny condemning the faults of the other. In both societies no measurable value is attributed to environmental assets or resources, which have been appropriated by the state. Instead, political decisions, informed by hunch, guesswork, lobbying and bureaucratic rent-seeking first over-allocate resources one way, then under-allocate them another, almost at random.

Typical of this approach is the land-use planning system, which has so marred the landscapes of Britain and other democracies in the last few decades.

State-sponsored environmental vandalism is not confined to the landscape, however. Many in the West deplore the state of wildlife conservation in developing countries where killing exotic animals creates more value than preserving them. Yet North Atlantic fish stocks are treated no better. In the majority of European and American waters, state regulation of fish harvesting allows for no sense of ownership or husbandry of stocks. The result is a free-for-all of wanton destruction, akin to elephant or tiger poaching in Africa and India. In striking contrast, where countries such as Iceland have worked to establish tradable property rights in deep sea fishing, stocks have been preserved and built up.

Ironically the Chinese are victims of their own relative virtue when it comes to one kind of species protection. Tigers have been bred successfully in farms in China with a view to harvesting for their bone products, and now number some 5,000. Yet the Western insistence on state solutions to environmental resource allocation means that the trade in tiger parts is banned. So as Chinese tiger farmers go bust and cannot afford to feed their starving charges, the last wild tigers are illegally poached in the state run 'reserves' of India.

This is not to say that the Chinese are blameless on environmental matters — far from it. The Chinese quest for headline economic growth means that property rights, and the husbandry that goes with them, are absent from environmental assets. Pollution, deforestation and the destruction of heritage are rife. Our point is just that these attributes are also prevalent in the democratic West.

* * *

The way that democracy is evolving has profound consequences for the institution of nationhood itself. The rise of the nation state was intertwined with the establishment of liberalism. It acted both as a natural unit of political accountability, and as a cultural incubator of liberal institutions. The roots of liberalism were founded in the challenge to the ruling dynastic monarchies of Europe. These claimed to draw their legitimacy at least as much from God as from popular consent, either directly or through papal sanction. It is true that some regimes sought strength from appealing to and encouraging the growth of national patriotism. For example, the Hundred Years War that began as a dynastic struggle became increasingly polarised along national lines, as did the Wars of Independence between England and Scotland. But in harnessing patriotic energy, dynasts eventually undermined their own position and encouraged the tender shoots of liberty. In claiming to represent a nation, monarchies were forced to invite national participation in the business of government, not least to raise finance. Public support of the dynasty was offered conditionally, in exchange for restrictions on the arbitrary powers of government, in the form of embryonic parliaments and laws to protect civil liberties. The evolving nation became not just the natural unit of political accountability through popular representation. It also acted as the cradle of the other institutions of liberty, which evolved differently from state to state as power ebbed and flowed between different interest groups. So the relationship between church, state and people became very different in neighbouring countries as close geographically to each other as Scotland, England, France and Holland.

The structure of parliaments, the establishment of universities, the codifications of laws, the hierarchy of courts and the way that property rights were defined all evolved separately from nation to nation. As with other features of national life, these vital institutions have been profoundly influenced by the character of the society that fostered them, just as they have in turn contributed to the evolution of the national character. The resulting imperfections and quirks in the make up of every nation go hand in hand with the deep rooted cultural affinity that gives them legitimacy in the eyes of the public and so makes them work. The point is that the strengths of liberal institutions are bound up with national culture and tradition, so the nation state plays an important role in underpinning a free society.

A free society can be compared to a nation-sized liberal club. Internally, the rules are limited, and members allowed to pursue their own interests and priorities. But the point of the club is that members by and large have an affinity to each other, and so behave in a broadly similar and compatible way, appreciating and respecting the quirks, conventions, unwritten rules and institutions that regulate life in the club. If they did not, or if differences emerge, then some members can leave to form a more congenial society. The flip side is that newcomers to the club are expected to conform to the norms of behaviour of existing members. In a club the size of a nation, those norms can be very varied. But if a sizeable proportion of the population does not feel comfortable with the prevailing culture, the legitimacy of the state and the power of the government to impose rules come into question. The relationship between the members of a club is not utilitarian; it is based on the shared affinity and attitude to the rules that constitute the club. To extend the analogy, a democratic state is by contrast more like a public limited company. Citizens, like shareholders, expect a dividend and have no need for affinity with the organisation. Indeed, they can merge, sell out, and take an activist interest in the direction of the company. Democracy has fundamentally altered the relationship between citizens and state.

The nation state, however liberal, is by its nature somewhat exclusive. And since the government of a nation state draws its legitimacy domestically, it has no necessary obligations to citizens of other polities. Indeed, taking undue account of the views of foreigners can actually put the actions of a government at fault, because it is appointed to act in the interests of its citizens alone. This was in contrast to the earlier internationalism of dynastic monarchies, with their transnational obligations of religious and family allegiance. It is important to realise that liberalism and nationhood go hand in hand. While liberal values might be universal in theory, in practice the success of institutions relies on being embedded in a national consciousness.

It seems a paradox to many modern minds that the liberal states of the nineteenth century intervened forcefully, and sometimes harshly, in their dealings with outside powers. This paradox lies at the root of modern criticism of the unilateralism of countries such as the United States, which in foreign affairs retains a strong liberal tradition of government accountability to the domestic electorate, and mistrust of international institutions and codes of conduct. Yet it is important to distinguish between raw nationalism, and the duties of a liberal state in its international dealings. Nationalism is a necessary but not a sufficient condition for liberalism. The rise of nationalism resulted in a breakdown of the old dynastic methods of international relations. Arguably it contributed to the frightful conflicts of the nineteenth and early twentieth centuries as governments such as Revolutionary France and Nazi Germany that drew on the nation as their source of legitimacy sought to assert themselves against their neighbours.

But in a free society, while government acts in foreign affairs only in the interests of the citizens who appoint it, it is itself subject to, rather than the arbiter, of their interests.

Since aggressive warfare is almost always counter to individual interest, not least because it requires the sequestration of vast resources to prosecute it, modern liberal governments tend to be essentially defensive in their prosecution of foreign policy, and sometimes even isolationist.

The United States, for example, has a strong tradition of non-interventionism which reigned supreme right up until the First World War, and then reasserted itself between the wars. It did engage in a number of conflicts against the British, the Spanish and the Mexicans, for example, but almost always in (admittedly robust) defence of trading or citizen interests.

The British spent the eighteenth and nineteenth centuries assembling an enormous Empire. But much of this was acquired in what was essentially virgin territory (or so it mistakenly seemed to the colonists) or else as a series of defensive measures against continental aggressors (as with the acquisition of French, Dutch and Spanish colonies). Even India was acquired through a piecemeal series of annexations and border conflicts whose origin lay in the protection of trading interests, and roused considerable disquiet and guilt among the conquerors.

Liberal states have a much better record on free trade as well. Countries such as Britain, the US and the Netherlands have periodically gone through protectionist phases. But because the interests of most individual citizens are best served by trade, there has always been internal pressure to open up to international markets. And of course reliance on trading links makes warfare even less attractive to the citizens of a free society. Liberal states tend to be peaceful states. The contrast with the behaviour of nationalist demagogues such as Napoleon or Hitler, or else pre-liberal dynasts such as the Ottoman or Russian empires, is stark.

The liberal nation state has several clear advantages as a unit of government. It encourages healthy, generally peaceful, competition between different societies that highlights successful practices, and encourages emulation in states that fall behind. The Western model is now copied (however imperfectly) throughout the world, and the success of northern European liberal societies such as England and Holland inspired political liberalism and industrial capitalism throughout Europe and beyond in the late eighteenth and nineteenth centuries.

Successful nation states can also grow by attracting immigrants who wish to buy into the liberal ethos. England acted as a haven for the persecuted minorities of Europe from early modern times, and the United States owes its size and power to mass immigration from Europe in the nineteenth and early twentieth centuries.

The advent of democratic socialism has undermined the proper functioning of nation states. The philosophies used to justify the growth of government in democracies are adverse to the particularism that is inherent to nationhood, and the liberal values that flourish within it.

A philosophy that seeks equality of outcomes necessarily rejects the liberal idea that a culture can regard itself as superior to others. The class struggle is mirrored in internationalism. This means that the process of evolutionary development in different states, where individual cultural and geographic characteristics lead to experimentation and specialisation, is regarded with suspicion. The notion that the successful liberal (or post-liberal) nations of the West have developed a superior model is disputed. And the suggestion that the values of Western liberalism are superior to, say, theocratic obscurantism, is denounced as racist. A kind of moral relativism flows from democratic socialism. Internally there is no virtue in thrift and hard work, because it demeans the unfortunate unemployed. To avoid discrimination every state of existence, every attitude and approach to life must be considered as equally valid. So the triumphs of the liberal West are downplayed and ignored. Alternative creeds are upheld, even if they explicitly reject the hard-won certainties of liberalism. It is almost as if the West is now ashamed of what it is and what made it great. Such an attitude, now commonplace in state education, government, the churches and even the military, saps the confidence of Westerners and their willingness to uphold liberal values.

At the same time, the quest for desirable economic and social outcomes means that the quirky interests of the state are relegated in the list of diplomatic priorities. Democratic socialists dislike the nation state, even though they derive their legitimacy from the people. They enter into alliances and join international conventions that undermine the sovereignty of the nation and the peculiar institutions that have evolved there. All this is detrimental to Western liberalism. The values and institutions that make liberal societies so successful are undermined. Modern democracies have forgotten, or reject, the idea of the nation as a liberal club. Since no culture is better or worse than any other, they actively pursue immigration policies without insisting that the newcomers accept the mores and evolved institutions of their hosts. This further undermines the self-confidence of Westerners who still hold to the liberal principles that made their countries great. Worse, it fractures the cohesive nation state, threatening to replicate and multiply the familiar problems of Lebanon or Northern Ireland across the cities and provinces of the West.

In a final irony, the Western states are beginning to shake off the shackles of the electoral mechanism itself. As we argued in Chapter One, elections are an important restriction on the power of the executive because they force an element of accountability on governments and act as a vehicle for political change. The problem is not with elections in themselves, therefore, but with the fact that the advent of democracy relegitimised government and undermined the other liberal institutions that underpinned Western freedoms. Now we see that Western governments are undermining this last limit on their power, the accountability function of democracy. The monster is turning on its creator. So self-confident has the state become in Western societies that it is even starting to repudiate the verdict of the electorate. In European politics particularly, it is increasingly common for governments to manipulate plebiscites and elections to validate policy decisions, or, where voters come up with the 'wrong' answer, to ignore the results of the vote and even arrange re-runs to get the required result.

At the same time, democratic governments love to bind themselves to unaccountable bureaucracies in the name of economic efficiency. Municipal government in Britain, for example, is now largely administered by an unelected bureaucracy, with only a nominal oversight role for elected councillors. Huge swathes of the social democratic state have been transferred to 'quangos', unelected bureaucracies in charge of everything from environmental regulation to 'heritage' to economic governance. Worse, democratic governments are ever more prone to transfer powers to supra-national bodies such as the European Union with only the most tenuous claims to electoral accountability. The EU started off with benign intentions. It was sold as a free market zone that had to be neutrally policed by a central agency. Yet the agency, unfettered by the long-evolved checks and balances of each member, has quickly acquired more powers, and imposed more rules and regulations, so that its economic costs now outweigh the advantages of free trade. Its *raison d'etre* is now political, and so inimical to liberal values. There is a clear parallel between the EU and the trans-national allegiances of pre-modern governments, overseen by the papacy and cemented by dynastic ties. Just as in the Middle Ages, European Governments are effectively in alliance with each other against the interests of their people. So the nation state, a crucial framework to the development of liberal institutions, is being dissolved. At home, society is fractured by the loss of mutual affinity, and abroad new structures of international bureaucracy undermine the nation's distinctiveness and its role as the natural unit of political accountability. In Chapter Three we discussed how democracy is self-defeating because it erodes the capacity of the citizen to take an active role in mature politics. Now we see that its contradictions go even further — the very electoral foundations of democracy are threatened by the powerful bureaucratic state that is its inevitable offspring.

* * *

Democracy is lending a new legitimacy to the state in Western societies, and the state is growing as a result. Consequently all of the liberal institutions which were the foundations of Western exceptionalism and the stunning intellectual and material success of Western societies are being undermined. In some areas the process is quicker than others, but there is a clear reversion to the pre-liberal situation where government is the final arbiter in peoples' lives, economically, legally, morally and intellectually.

In space and time, this is the normal condition of human societies, and so the West is simply reverting to the normal trend of history. The liberal era was a blip. It was a fluke that may not be repeated. It should be no surprise when the pattern of history resumes along the lines that it usually follows. It is always dangerous to draw historical parallels between one era and another. But we have seen this trend before at the end of the classical era. Taking the example of ancient Rome is useful as an illustration of what can happen in human societies, and so can help open our eyes to our current predicament.

The Roman Republic was very different from the modern West, but had certain institutional similarities, some of which became models for the liberal architects of our own societies. Roman politicians drew their legitimacy from an electoral process, but the constitution was replete with checks and balances designed to restrict the power of the executive. Just like the modern West, the Romans learnt to limit the power of their own tyrannical monarchy. These included one year terms for the senior magistracy (the consulship), which was itself split between two co-heads of state. Legislative power rested with a popular assembly, with the senate (consisting of current and previous elected officials) advising the consuls. The Romans were also very proud of their legal system as a bulwark against arbitrary power. The rule of law allowed a relatively sophisticated system of commercial contracts and trade to exist. The system was not proof against politicians redistributing the wealth of the growing empire to secure electoral support among the poor. And indeed political competition combined with questions of welfare and the need for an ever more professional army to destabilise the constitution fatally, resulting in the permanent dictatorship of Julius Caesar and his successors.

But while the process by which the state threw off its constitutional shackles differed from the modern West, the effects were somewhat similar. Imperial Rome witnessed the growth of the state's arbitrary power, and the cowing of civil society. The sole purpose of the Empire became the maintenance of the governmental edifice, propped up by an ever more dominant army. Taxation and regulation increased and commerce and urban life suffered. By the fourth and fifth centuries, the Roman government was imposing ever heavier and more punitive regulations to force citizens to undertake activities that had previously been performed voluntarily — whether to farm certain tracts of land, perform military duties or maintain civic buildings. The stagnation of the empire's economy and society played a big role in its collapse. It started to resemble its supposedly barbarian neighbours to the North.

In the same way, the West is losing the exceptional institutional structures that gave it such an advantage over its competitors. The liberal age was one where essentially the state had no agenda of its own. It simply acted as a framework within which civil society could develop and flourish with little guiding force. Such freedom allowed ingenuity, imagination, and productivity. With the demise of liberalism the West is reverting to the mainstream of history, where states compete by deploying resources in a quest for power.

In an information age, technological advantage is fleeting, and in a democratic age, institutional advantages are eroded. Geopolitics therefore simply becomes a question of human resources. Whichever state can harness their population most effectively has the advantage. There was a brief moment in the rise of the West when it was technologically similar to civilisations it encountered such as the Ottoman Empire. The Ottoman state was adept at deploying raw manpower resources, and so remained militarily threatening until the West's institutional structures allowed it to deploy new technology to deliver permanent material advantages. The pre-liberal era, where power politics was a reflection of which state could deploy more of its citizens to further its objectives is surely returning. And as the relative power of the West declines, so the process will hasten as other models seem just as successful, and the vestiges of liberalism lose their attractiveness.

This is not to say that some barbarous new dark age of warfare and conquest is imminent. With the end of liberalism, warfare may be more likely, but the destructive power of modern warfare may yet hold back the despots. The West will not necessarily 'fall' in a cataclysmic conflict. But it will be transformed. The process will be gradual. Just as it has taken a hundred years for the nature of democracy to become manifest, so it will be another hundred before the institutional advantages that liberalism bestowed upon the West are fully dissipated.

When that happens, in terms of power politics, Western countries will be no more powerful than their equivalents in population terms elsewhere in the world. And those countries with the greatest manpower will dominate. At the same time as its institutions are undermined, so will the distinctive culture of the West be eroded under the tides of internationalism.

Night will come, but it will be a gentle, prolonged sunset. As to the following dawn, who can predict the next accident of history when mankind will once more throw off the shackles of big government?

Epilogue

An Idea for the Future

Our argument has been that the West is doomed to a gradual decline as the pressures of democratic socialism gradually erode the liberal foundation of the West's political and economic success. Efforts to control the arbitrary use of power in society have been systematically undermined by the idea that democracy legitimises state action and provides an egalitarian moral ideal that should direct the actions of the state. We are pessimistic about the chances of reversing these trends. The power of government in Western society has expanded enormously, and it seems most unlikely that our politicians can be persuaded to relinquish it. And democracy has an inherent stability in that it enjoys the acquiescence of the majority. Too many are beneficiaries (in the short term) of the munificence of the state.

If the West is condemned to revert to tyranny, however, sooner or later we can hope for a new liberal resurgence. This may not happen for many years, and will perhaps take place in a different part of the world altogether. And just as the modern liberals sought to build on and improve upon the example of the ancients, this new breed of freedom lovers will no doubt learn from our experience. What will their conclusions be, and what will they seek to do differently from us?

First of all they will understand why the West has been successful in providing the greatest individual liberty and the greatest level of material wealth ever enjoyed thus far in human history. They will gain intellectual confidence in the ideas of liberalism as a force for human progress. They will reawaken the mistrust of politics and the potential abuse of political power that characterised liberalism and see through the false sheen of legitimacy that democracy throws on the use of coercion in society. But it will be immediately apparent that the old liberal tools intended to limit the activities of the state failed to check the cycle of democratic socialism in our era. The written constitutions, with checks and balances, the independent judiciary, Bills of Rights and regular elections have all failed to protect individuals from activist politicians. Each have played a part in the liberal project and must have their place in any future revival of liberty, but they are clearly not enough on their own.

The essential flaw in liberal institutions is that while they may delay the growth of the power of the state, they do not limit it absolutely. So while the checks and balances introduced by, say, the division of power, make it harder for the executive to pass laws, they do not prevent them. Over time, therefore, the quantity of laws and regulations still increases, and some of those laws are inevitably directed by activist politicians at undermining other liberal institutions such as the independent judiciary or civil liberties. However, attempts to impose hard and fast limits on the quantity or scope of legislation would be inflexible and invite attempts to break those limits. Perhaps the only hope for liberalism is to acknowledge the forces at play in a democracy and seek to contain them. Both the Roman Republic and the modern liberal states fell prey in the end to ambitious politicians who sought to break free from the constitutional trammels placed upon them.

A new liberal approach might seek to place finite limits on the power of the executive while granting leeway to human political ambition. What this might involve is using the natural process of time to limit the total body of law and the scope of government action. So laws would be time-limited in their effect, expiring automatically after a defined period. There is a powerful democratic as well as liberal justification for this in that we should not be bound by the rules of past legislators who by definition have no current electoral mandate. A refinement of this concept would be that the lifespan of a law would depend on the majority by which it was passed. Complex, divisive or far reaching measures would be limited in impact by their own controversy. But there would still be scope for decisive and lasting political action so long as it concurred with a broad consensus among the electorate. It would give some leeway to the natural ambitions of politicians who might otherwise seek to break the system. The result would be a finite body of law that nonetheless had the flexibility to deal with changing circumstances. The energies of our lawmakers would be directed in large part to reforming and improving the legal code rather than forever building upon it.

A similar principle could be applied to the economic power of the executive in terms of its ability to tax and own assets. Budgets that proposed levels of taxation above a certain minimum would require ever higher majorities to be passed. A talented political leader, in tune with the general will of his citizenry, and with a good cause, would still have considerable scope for action. But as the crisis receded, or the debate became more balanced, the state's ability to sequestrate the wealth of others would naturally subside.

Both of these concepts, of finite limits to the actions of the state, are tentatively being explored by modern liberals. 'Sunset clauses' — as time limits on laws are sometimes called — have even been implemented in some Western jurisdictions in a few areas. The idea of limits to the economic powers the state has been discussed in detail by political economists such as the Swede Knut Wicksell.

It is probably too much to hope that the West can save itself by implementing these measures in our own era. But at least in its decline it may have thrown up ideas that will germinate in the future. The West may fall, but hopefully its achievements will not be wholly in vain.

Bibliography

Aristotle *Politics*, trans. E. Barker, Oxford University Press, 1995.

Blair, T. *The Courage of our Convictions –Why reform of the public services is the route to social justice*, Fabian Ideas No. 603, 2002.

Bolingbroke, H. St John Viscount, *Political Writings*, ed. D. Armitage, Cambrdige University Press, 1997.

Buchanan, J.M. & Tullock, G. *The Calculus of Consent*, Liberty Fund, 1999.

De Jasay, A. 'Inspecting the Foundations of Liberalism', *Economic Affairs* Vol. 30, no. 1, March 2010, pp. 6-12.

De Soto, H. *The Mystery of Capital*, Basic Books, 2003.

Ferguson, A. *An Essay of the History of Civil Society*, ed. F. Oz-Salzberger, Cambridge University Press, 1994.

Friedman, M. & R. *The Tyranny of the Status Quo*, Penguin Books, 1985.

Hayek, F.A. *Law, Legislation and Liberty*, Routledge, 1982.

Hume, D. *Essays Moral Political and Literary*, ed. E.F. Miller, Liberty Fund, 1985.

Hutton, W. *The State We're In*, Vintage Books, 1996.

Madison, J., Hamilton, A. & Jay, J *The Federalist Papers*, ed. I. Kramnick, Penguin Books, 1987.

Mill, J.S. *On Liberty and Other Essays*, ed. J. Gray, Oxford University Press, 1991.

Montesquieu, Charles Louis de Secondat, *The Spirit of the Laws*, ed. A.M. Cohler, B.C. Miller & H.S. Stone, Cambridge University Press, 1989.

Plato *The Republic*, trans. Desmond Lee, Penguin Books, 1974.

Plato *The Laws*, trans. T.J. Saunders, Penguin Books, 1970.

Price, R. *Political Writings*, ed. D.O. Thomas, Cambridge University Press, 1991.

Rousseau, J-J. 'The Social Contract', in E. Barker ed. *Social Contract*, Oxford University Press, 1960.

Smith, A. *An Inquiry into the Nature and Causes of the Wealth of Nations*, ed. T. Campbell, A. Skinner & W. Todd, Oxford University Press, 1976.

Wicksell, K 'A New Principle of Just Taxation' in R. Musgrave & A. Peacock eds. *Classics in the Theory of Public Finance*, Macmillan, 1967.